Writers of Wales

Dorothy Edwards

Writers of Wales

Dorothy Edwards

Claire Flay

University of Wales Press

Cardiff 2011

www.uwp.co.uk

British Library Cataloguing-in-Publication Data
A catalogue record for this book is available from the British Library.

ISBN 978-0-7083-2440-0
e-ISBN 978-0-7083-2441-7

The publisher acknowledges the financial support of the Welsh Books Council.

Typeset in Wales by Eira Fenn Gaunt, Fenn Typesetting, Cardiff
Printed in Wales by Dinefwr Press, Llandybïe

For Aneira

Contents

Acknowledgements

I am indebted to several people and institutions for their help in preparing this book. My primary thanks go to Jane Aaron, who not only has read through innumerable versions of this manuscript and has made invaluable suggestions for improvement and amendment, but has also provided me with significant support and encouragement during my research on Dorothy Edwards. I am also very grateful to Diana Wallace for her guidance with this project in its initial format as a Ph.D. thesis. For their unwavering support and encouragement I would like to thank Jonathan Petty, and Ceri and Anthony Flay.

I am indebted to the University of Reading Special Collections, and in particular Verity Andrews, for their kind assistance in accessing the original manuscript material that underpins this volume, and for granting permission to quote from the Dorothy Edwards Archives (MS5085) and to reproduce the photograph of Edwards which forms the cover image of this book. I am also grateful to: Tony Brown, Christopher Meredith and Luned Meredith for conversations that helped focus my thoughts and arguments about Edwards; the Ogmore Valley Local History and Heritage Society, and Huw Daniel and William (Bert) Jones in particular, for invaluable information on Edward Edwards and Ogmore Vale; and Dr Marion Löffler at the Centre for Advanced Welsh and Celtic Studies, National Library of Wales, for her translation of Walter von der Vogelweide's 'Lob des Winters'.

I am grateful to the following for permission to use their work/records: Richard Garnett, for allowing me to make use of and quote from the Dorothy Edwards/David Garnett correspondence, now held in the Garnett Family Archive at Charles Deering McCormick

Library of Special Collections, Northwestern University Library, and David Garnett's *The Familiar Faces* (London: Chatto & Windus, 1962); Emrys Evans, for having the foresight to preserve the documentation that now forms the Dorothy Edwards Archives, held at the University of Reading Special Collections, for his permission to quote from this material, and for information on S. Beryl Jones and Winifred Kelly; the Glamorgan Archives, for allowing me access to the Tynewydd School logbooks (E/M/55/6); Luned Meredith and Gwen Davies, for permission to quote from the Glyn Jones correspondence; Charles Deering McCormick Library of Special Collections, Northwestern University Library, for permission to reproduce the photograph of Dorothy Edwards from the Garnett Family Archive; and King's College Library, Cambridge, and Gill Coleridge of Rogers, Coleridge and White literary agents for permission to use the photograph of Dorothy Edwards and David Garnett (FCP-7-4-2-101 Dorothy Edwards and FCP-7-4-2-102 Dorothy Edwards and David Garnett).

I would also like to thank the University of Wales Press, and in particular Sarah Lewis for her patient advice and guidance. The Ph.D. research that forms the basis of this book could not have been conducted without initial support from the James Pantyfedwen Foundation, Aberystwyth, and a doctoral award from the Arts and Humanities Research Council.

Illustrations

The picture section is placed between pages 82–83

Cover image: Dorothy Edwards. Reproduced with kind permission of University of Reading, Special Collections, Dorothy Edwards Archive (MS5085).

1   Dorothy Edwards aged 9, 1913. The text on the verso of this photograph reads 'With love to Mama from Dorothy for her Birthday. May 13 1913.' Reproduced with kind permission of Richard Garnett and Charles Deering McCormick Library of Special Collections, Northwestern University Library.

2   Edward Edwards's gravestone. The inscription reads: 'This book was laid by the Tynewydd Ward Labour Party, the Trade Unions & the Cooperative Society. In memory of Edward Edwards, Schoolmaster & Socialist Pioneer.'

3   Dorothy Edwards and David Garnett (c.1930) at Hamspray House. Reproduced with kind permission of Gill Coleridge of Rogers, Coleridge and White, and King's College Library, Cambridge.

4   Dorothy Edwards (c.1930) at Hamspray House. Reproduced with kind permission of Gill Coleridge of Rogers, Coleridge and White, and King's College Library, Cambridge.

Abbreviations

R	Dorothy Edwards, *Rhapsody* (1927; Cardigan: Parthian, 2007)
WS	Dorothy Edwards, *Winter Sonata* (1928; London: Virago, 1986)
GA	Glamorgan Archives
DEA	Dorothy Edwards Archive (MS5085), University of Reading, Special Collections
GFA	Garnett Family Archive, Charles Deering McCormick Library of Special Collections, Northwestern University Library

From Brynteg to Pen-y-dre: Dorothy Edwards in Ogmore Vale and Rhiwbina

In a 1925 essay which she contributed to the then University College of South Wales and Monmouthshire's (now Cardiff University) magazine *Cap and Gown*, Dorothy Edwards described the difficulties she experienced as a budding author:

> Now I thought of a wonderful story the day before yesterday, which would have made this Magazine sell like hot bricks, but unluckily, it was very important that my hero should cash a cheque. Now, up to this point in my career, it has never been necessary for me to cash a cheque, and half-way through the story, I found to my horror that I did not know what happened . . . so I had to abandon it.[1]

Her problem, she explained, stemmed from her inability to follow the standard line of advice to would-be authors, to 'write about what you know': her own lack of life experience making it difficult to do so. 'You must be a realist or you must invent a personal isolated odd universe composed exclusively of your own experience', Edwards wrote in a letter to her close friend S. Beryl Jones.[2] Edwards chose the latter. The world in which she locates her fiction could not be more different from the south Wales coal-mining community in which she was born and raised, or the respectable but impoverished life that she later led in the Cardiff suburb of Rhiwbina. Her stories are usually narrated from a male perspective and are set in large country houses or holiday retreats where her middle- and upper-class characters spend idle lives or long summer vacations. They do not worry about everyday needs and are generally financially independent, unlike the characters of her Welsh contemporaries, as author Glyn Jones has pointed out: '[u]sually in Anglo-Welsh writing the only people who do not work are the ones on the dole'.[3] Given the setting and tone of Edwards's fiction, her readers could be forgiven for initially believing hers to be the work of a middle-class male author.

What Edwards created in her fiction was a world at once removed from and yet permeated with her experiences, her passions, her politics and her outlook on life. Music, her greatest love, infiltrates all its aspects, from the titles of her two publications, to her characters' abilities; references to various composers, songs, operas and technical terms abound in her 1927 short story collection *Rhapsody*, and the structure of her 1928 novel *Winter Sonata* is based, as the title suggests, on the sonata form. Likewise, myth and legend, particularly that of Greek origin, underpin the plots of her stories and her novel. While she avoided describing the minutiae of everyday life, the sparse and pared down tone of her writing is influenced by the Russian and European literature that she so greatly admired (Leo Tolstoy, Fyodor Dostoevsky and Knut Hamsun received particular praise in her letters). A sense of exclusion, of isolation, of loneliness dominates. Several of Edwards's stories feature young women, just out of school, trying to find their place in the world. The motherless Primrose in 'Mutiny', for example, spends four years in boarding school, the effect of which seems only to have sharpened her sense of the attractions of upper-class culture and leads her from the custody of one man to another. Edwards's female characters are forced into teaching, marriage or an idle drawing-room life. Bonds between women are largely absent. Parental responsibility is lacking: children are usually missing one or both parents, and there are few mothers in her stories. All of these features can be related to her own experiences. Most of all, Edwards's fiction is permeated with an awareness of power structures which, as a young Welsh woman, dominated her life.

Edwards has in the past been more generally known for the tragic circumstances surrounding her suicide in 1934 at the age of thirty-one, than for the literary value of her work and its relevance to Wales, largely as a result of her unusual choice of subject matter. Arguments concerning the validity of representations of Wales have been inherently gender-based, underpinned by the suggestion that writing by Welsh men is somehow truer of the Welsh experience than writing by Welsh women. In her extensive and groundbreaking research on Welsh women's history, Deirdre Beddoe suggests that the very specific formations of Welsh society have rendered 'Welsh women . . . culturally invisible'.[4] Historically, there has been little room to negotiate a place for women in Welsh cultural consciousness. As Beddoe points out, the dominant stereotypical signifiers of Welsh popular culture during the last 150 or so years have been overtly masculine. The dominance of heavy industry in Wales and the significance that this industry has come to have in Welsh cultural consciousness means that much writing from Wales has been centred upon issues relating to the coalfield and its workers in terms of both content and style. Economics, labour politics and employment are all key features of work by the likes of Merthyr Tydfil author Jack Jones and Rhondda-based writers Lewis Jones and Gwyn Thomas. Anglo-Welsh writing, for much of the twentieth century at least, became synonymous with male industrial fiction of the south Wales valleys. The gritty, realist narrative that characterizes the work of the male valleys writers could not be further removed from the middle-class country houses and tense, claustrophobic relationships that form the focus of Dorothy Edwards's fiction. As a result, Glyn Jones felt that Edwards was 'too remote – not a Welsh writer in English' and so did not 'take much interest in her'.[5] Edwards 'comes nearest to those writers who deal with artistic people at their week-ends in the country' he commented in *The Dragon Has Two Tongues*.[6] Twentieth-century Welsh writing in English is dominated by its engagement with industry, labour and class conflict, and the way in which these created and contributed to a specifically Welsh national identity; by failing to set her work in Wales, Edwards, it seems, was not considered quite Welsh enough.

On the whole, the fiction privileged as truly representative of Wales did not begin to emerge until after Edwards's death in 1934: prior to the 1930s, the industrial landscape was yet to be interpreted in any significant detail in English-language Welsh prose. As Katie Gramich points out in her comparative essay on Edwards and Kate Roberts,

Mil naw tri saith oedd y trobwynt, mae'n debyg, gyda sefydlu'r cylch-grawn *Wales*, a alluogoedd awduron di-Gymraeg Cymru i anelu eu gwaith yn uniongyrchol at ddarllenwyr Cymreig.[7]

(The year 1937 was the turning point, it seems, with the establishment of the magazine *Wales*, enabling non-Welsh-speaking Welsh authors to aim their work directly at the Welsh reader.)

The only Welsh writer making a successful attempt at industrial-based fiction before 1930 was Rhys Davies: writing in London in the 1920s, Davies set his fiction in the Rhondda of his upbringing and focused on the lives of those connected with the coalfield. His first novel, *The Withered Root* (1927), appeared in the same year as *Rhapsody*. But, as Tony Brown has pointed out, Davies was a full-time writer living in London by the time he began publishing his work, and wrote about Wales from the point of view of an exile.[8] Furthermore, Davies's living arrangements left him free to pursue his writing in a manner that Edwards could not. Although he often found himself living in near poverty while in London, Davies experienced a degree of freedom and independence that, as a writer, Edwards was never able to enjoy. By and large, Edwards was writing and publishing her work in an atmosphere in which Welsh writing was still mostly required to be romantic, or at best parochial, in order to be considered commercially viable. The success of Welsh writer Allen Raine[9] proves a case in point: while Raine was highly aware of the social and economic factors affecting her Welsh communities, and portrays these with accuracy and skill, her novels are at times melodramatic, involving several central characters intertwined in intricate and often unrealistic plots. Raine published her first novel, *A Welsh Singer*, in 1897; by 1911, her novels, two of which were made into silent films, had sold over two million copies.[10] Her books were read in America, the British colonies and Australia (the above sales figures exclude the American market); at various times during the eighty years following her death they were translated into Irish, French and Welsh.[11] This led John Harris, in his 1993 article on Raine, to claim that '[w]hatever the judgement of literary historians, for the book trade Anglo-Welsh literature unquestionably began in 1897 with the publication of *A Welsh Singer*'.[12] Edwards's work, stripped of any explicit reference to Wales and devoid even of a Welsh setting, came to be read for all intents and purposes as 'English'. A close study of Edwards's fiction, however, reveals that she in fact developed a mode of writing that explored in a very specific way the power dynamics of her society as she saw it.

Dorothy Edwards was born on 18 August 1903 to Edward and Vida Edwards, of Brynteg, Glyn Street, in the small mining community of Ogmore Vale, south Wales. The family lived in a large, semi-detached, white-painted house, on which 'the coal dust from the colliery near[by] descended without cease'.[13] Both Vida and Edward had come to the Ogmore valley, separately, to teach. They met in 1896 when Vida was appointed to the position of headmistress of the infants' section of the English-medium Tynewydd Infants and Juniors Mixed School in Ogmore Vale, where Edward Edwards had acted as headmaster since 1894.[14] They married in 1899, when both were in their late thirties, and Dorothy was their first and only child. In her 1933 diary, now held in the Dorothy Edwards Archives at the University of Reading, Edwards describes a photograph of her parents taken around the time of her birth:

> They are seated in a garden with an old oak tree as a background. My mother is doing a piece of embroidery and has on a blouse with a paisley pattern, of which long afterwards I made dresses for my dolls. My father has his legs crossed and a pair of resplendent golf stockings with ornament tops adorn them [*sic*]. He has his head a little to one side as he looks straight at the camera with a contented and profoundly happy smile. My mother's head with its dark curly hair is bent over a piece of embroidery as though she does not really know that she is being taken. They are both so good looking, and so much in love, and the scene with its old tree and the garden benches & the wall behind is so charming that I am distressed to find at the side of the picture spoiling its symmetry and grace a baby in a silk dress and a little bonnet with a most discontented & perplexed expression on its face, who must be myself.[15]

Edwards paints an attractive picture of her parents: they are confident, happy, relaxed. But she sees herself as a blot on the scene, at once a part of her parents and cut off from them. Rather than being an indication of her parents' feelings towards her, this passage reflects the personal sense of separation and isolation that is embodied in her writing.

By the time of Dorothy's birth in 1903, Edward Edwards had been a headmaster in the valley for thirteen years.[16] He is remembered as an eccentric figure in the community: a vegetarian, a Sunday golfer, an ardent socialist and Independent Labour Party leader, his political views influenced his actions both personally and professionally. In all likelihood it was his influence with the highly successful Co-operative movement of the valley (he kept the books) that inspired the local branch in January 1904 to send 320 oranges to the school for distribution among the pupils.[17] At the height of the 1911 miners' strike, a canteen committee was formed in the school to feed 'the children of strikers and other children in need'; superintended by Edward Edwards, the scheme provided meals for 130 children a day, and was continued in the Easter holiday when the meals were paid for by voluntary funds.[18] In 1975, a former secretary of Tynewydd School recalled: 'Mr Edwards is remembered even today as being quite a character. He was reputed to be a nudist and he used to camp out on the mountainside near an old well.'[19]

In her 1933 diary, Edwards later recorded that a free communion with nature was not her father's aim here; his 'nudism' was merely a part of his method of testing his socialist beliefs. She wrote:

Now since the socialist text books of those days were much given to describing utopias, & my father had a practical mind he decided to test in his own life what minimum of luxury and sophistication was necessary to a man of the industrial age, one summer he divested himself of everything but his clothes and went to live in a cave on the mountain top in a beautiful little ravine. And when he got there, he took off his clothes too, so that my mother taking her friends on occasion to picnic in his company [*deleted* – would as she approached have to call loudly and urgently to announce their arrival, so] would have to announce their approach by calling loudly and urgently to him [*deleted* – in a voice] to indicate that he must put on at least a towel to receive them. Very soon he discovered that he needed a hatchet and a frying pan and as Autumn approached he built a fine fire place & acquired a tent, so that the Socialist street corner orators who stayed so often in our house were able to observe primitive man to whom they loved to refer in their speeches, in the various stages of his evolution.[20]

In his mountain-top camp Edward Edwards proceeded to hold meetings with his socialist friends, many of whom were major political figures in the area at the time, to which young Dorothy was privy. '[B]eside our camp fire we proudly entertained Keir Hardie, Bruce Glasier, Stitt Wilson, [Robert] Smillie & [George] Lansbury,' she later recalled.[21] Greatly influenced by her father's progressive and unconventional practices and beliefs, Dorothy too proclaimed herself to be a socialist and became a lifelong member of the Independent Labour Party at a very young age. According to David Garnett, in later life one of Edwards's fondest childhood recollections was that of welcoming Hardie on to the stage in Tonypandy during the 1912 miners' strike when she was nine years old, dressed from head to toe in red.[22] Despite Edward Edwards's position as a white-collar worker, he was evidently concerned with the well-being of his mining neighbours. Edwards recalls one occasion when his concerns caused her mother some public embarrassment:

[O]nce when, having been long disturbed by the thought of the number of his miner friends who worked with their feet in water, he saw advertised a pair of steel-soled boots of no very elegant cut, and they arrived just as he was taking her to the cinema, she had to support the embarrassment of emerging from the front door and walking along the crowded street with him plodding delightedly behind her and of hearing him thunder upon the iron edged steps of the Workmen's hall as he followed her up the stairs to the best seats. And he wore these terrible boots every day to school until they were thoroughly advertised & the address of the maker passed round.[23]

The beliefs held by her father had a huge impact on Edwards's life and her perception of society. In one of the most self-reflective passages of her 1933 diary, which is dedicated to the Canadian socialist and contemporary of Edward Edwards, J. Stitt Wilson, she wrote:

I have been much luckier than most people . . . I benefited by my father's progressive ideas on education. Over and above this I learnt to ask for what I had a right to; from the great Socialists whom I knew when I was little, you among them. All this was a sheer gift that life made to me and to how few others! . . . How about the young artists, thinkers, great souls, who are not armed against the world beforehand by knowing Keir Hardie or you?[24]

Dorothy Edwards's mother, Vida, has previously had little or no mention in the few biographical accounts of Edwards, obscured as she was by her husband's eccentricities as much as the social conventions of her time. Until her marriage in 1899, Vida had a successful career as headteacher of the infants' section of Tynewydd School. Despite resigning from her post on her marriage (her career, like that of so many women, was a victim of the legislation barring married women from working as teachers),[25] she often took charge of the school in her husband's absence long after she had resigned from any official capacity, and there is no suggestion that any of the other teachers, or indeed parents, felt that this was inappropriate.[26] Vida was also apparently active in the socialist community: records of the Women's Labour League suggest that she was involved in the pithead baths campaign, of which Edward Edwards certainly would have approved.[27]

But Vida struggled to maintain the family's social image while supporting the more extreme of her husband's views that she, apparently, did not share. Edward Edwards had clearly made a name for himself as a controversial, albeit progressive, headmaster; the burden of his eccentricities, however, seems to have fallen wholly on his wife's shoulders. '[S]he had to accept the discordant note of my father's red tie, of which indeed I think she came to understand the vital necessity', recalled Edwards.[28] During her husband's socialist experiments on the mountainside, Vida

remained in the valley below, and made tea for the committees and bore in agony the jeers of the passers by when her husband, come back to civilisation for the occasion, stood on our kitchen chair on the waste-ground next to the police station, and tried to collect a crowd for the coming meeting.[29]

Dazzled by the light of her father's radicalism, Edwards saw her mother by comparison as conventional and staid. She recalls that Vida expended 'much anxiety and pain upon the difficult task of reconciling her husband's revolutionary views with the obvious respectability and merit of the wondering friends and relations, who disagreed with him so emphatically'.[30] Edwards writes:

> [M]y mother with heroic [sic] defended him in her polite tea-drinkings with [deleted – the wives of doctors & colliery managers] the most distinguished society of the place; learned to cook the most [deleted – incredible] unheard of dishes which he delighted to pass off on his carnivorous friends as the accustomed fish or flesh; and sat in chapel through Welsh sermons which were not without pointed references to sinners who played games on the Lord's Day upon the mountain tops.[31]

As Tony Brown has suggested, Edwards, like her contemporaries Rhys Davies, Glyn Jones and Alun Lewis, was set apart from the rest of the community as a result of her father's occupation.[32] Despite Edward Edwards's political and social sympathies, he had a clean, safe and comparatively well-paid and secure job, and having only one child meant little strain on the household in terms of finance or space. While Edwards was learning about politics from her father and his friends, her female contemporaries in the valley were being raised to be the wives and mothers of future working-class generations, and this further contributed to Edwards's removal from the community in which she was born and raised. As her formal education progressed, this ideological displacement became physical.

The circumstances of Edwards's early education are unclear. The autobiographical recollections of a contemporary, Rachael Ann Webb, who was raised in Ogmore Vale during the same period as Edwards, recalls a playground friendship in the valley's infant school with a girl named Dorothy who 'took her own life when she was in her thirties'.[33] Claims that Edwards was later educated in the boys' school in which her father taught are misleading, as fascinating as this would be, in terms of Edwards's sense of displacement and her use of a male voice in her fiction. While Edward Edwards was indeed the headmaster of the boys' section of Tynewydd School, male and female pupils shared the same school building. Tynewydd Boys' School, with Edward Edwards as its headmaster, was not established until 1915, by which time Edwards was almost certainly a pupil at Ogmore Grammar School.[34] But Edwards was not to remain in the valley education system for long: on 19 September 1916, at the age of thirteen, she enrolled as a scholarship boarder at the prestigious Howell's School for Girls, Llandaff.

As an only child, with a strong socialist background, in a private, fee-paying school forty miles away from home, Edwards's sense of displacement in Howell's must have been acute. The death of her father when Edwards was in her second year at Howell's only exacerbated her sense of rootlessness. Edward Edwards had been ill for some time, suffering from a debilitating disease that led to frequent absences from his teaching post, before his death on 22 December 1917.[35] His funeral took place on Boxing Day 1917. The *Glamorgan Gazette* reported on his funeral, describing him as 'the well-known Welsh I.L.P. leader' who

> was justly respected for his fearless independence in expressing his opinions and his courage in fighting on behalf of weak causes from which he could never hope to obtain any material reward beyond the satisfaction of having acted on conviction and from a sense of duty.[36]

At his burial, family and friends were joined not only by representatives of the local collieries, schools and workingmen's clubs, but by members of the south Wales branches of the Independent Labour Party, the Miners' Federation, the National Union of Teachers and the Co-operative Society.[37] Edward Edwards was evidently well respected in his locality. Shortly before his death, he had received an address and a cheque 'in recognition of his public services', and on his grave in Ogmore Vale cemetery sits a large stone, book-shaped monument, which reads: 'This book was laid by the Tynewydd Ward Labour Party, the Trade Unions & the Cooperative Society. In memory of Edward Edwards, Schoolmaster & Socialist Pioneer.'[38] Edward Edwards's death inevitably had a huge impact on his wife and daughter not only emotionally, but practically. Barely a month after his death, Vida took up a full-time teaching post in her late husband's school. Here she remained for eighteen months until, in March 1919, she was transferred to Ely School in Cardiff, and the family left Ogmore Vale for good.[39]

Dorothy Edwards's move from the industrialized, labour-orientated valley community, which in effect began with her removal to Howell's school in 1916, was now all but complete, signifying not only a split from the world of her father but also from the working class with which the family, ideologically at least, associated themselves. In Cardiff, Vida and Edwards rented number 9, Pen-y-dre, in the garden village of Rhiwbina, where they found themselves, to all intents and purposes, among the bourgeoisie.[40] But Edwards endeavoured to remain true to her father's socialist teaching. Harold Watkins, who became a long-standing family friend, first met Edwards at a socialist rally shortly after her move to Rhiwbina, where she was reciting a William Morris poem for the occasion.[41] Watkins describes 17-year-old Edwards as 'pretty in spite of projecting teeth, well developed, free of self-consciousness, [and] unusually vivacious'.[42]

From Howell's, Edwards enrolled as an undergraduate student of Greek and philosophy at the University College of South Wales and Monmouthshire in 1920 where she soon became part of a circle of intelligent, ambitious and unconventional young women. S. Beryl Jones, who remained Edwards's closest friend for the rest of her life, had an active interest in politics and a similar background to Edwards, having been born and raised in an English-speaking Welsh family in a working-class community in Resolven. Like Edwards, Jones's father's white-collar position as a mining engineer meant that the family was, essentially, middle class, and Jones too had been a pupil at Howell's.[43] But by the end of the First World War Mr Jones had lost his job, and the political climate leading up to the General Strike in 1926 'led Beryl to a markedly left-wing political position'.[44] Winifred Kelly, another very close friend of Edwards, later became a lecturer at University College of Wales Aberystwyth and contributed regularly to the *Welsh Review*.[45] Sona Rosa Burstein, who had struck up a friendship with Edwards in Cardiff which was later rekindled in the 1930s in London, went on to become a distinguished anthropologist and an expert on witch-craft.

Edwards relished university life, and her letters from this time are light-hearted, energetic and engaging. She wrote for the college magazine *Cap and Gown*, and became involved in a variety of extra-mural events. Watkins remembers her as a 'gay, carefree student'.[46] Her passion for music and drama found an outlet in the university's dramatic society (she acted in several of its productions). For much of her life she had desired above all else to become an opera singer: she received singing lessons while a student, and for a time she intended after graduating to further cultivate her talent in Milan. Watkins claims that Edwards was 'taught by one of the most success-ful teachers in Wales' and that her singing, 'distinguished by artistry and intelligence', led her friends to think that 'she could have made a career out of it'.[47] Edwards apparently shared this sentiment: she wrote to Beryl Jones commenting: 'If I can save £250 Mother will lend me £500 & I can go to Milan – so my future is assured . . . I am feeling quite sure of my voice . . . Do you think I can save £250 by the time I am 26 or 27?'[48] Edwards also excelled academically: she gave papers to both the philosophical society and the English society, and her Greek lecturer Kathleen Freeman 'was impressed by the ease and rapidity with which she mastered the language . . . and still more by her appreciation of and insight into Greek litera-ture'.[49] Gilbert Norwood, professor of Greek, described Edwards as 'extremely well-read in contemporary literature, not only English, and is an excellent critic'. '[C]onstantly impressed by the skilful elegance of her own English style', Norwood evidently had a sense of Edwards's future career.[50]

Edwards made an equally strong, albeit different, impact on her philosophy lecturer John Thorburn, to whom she became engaged briefly. Time spent together in the classroom was supplemented by their active involvement in the philosophical society, and her letters to Jones and Kelly from this time are full of references to Thorburn.[51] When their short-lived engagement was broken off, her flippant comments do little to hide the real pain that she experienced. She wrote to Jones:

John is behaving abominably . . . I weep all weekends, so that I always feel happy on Mondays . . . He said I pushed him into it . . . I've just sent him a note in return for his request that he might 'serve' me in any way he could, assuring him that the only way would be to let me horsewhip him.[52]

Winifred Kelly's footnote to this letter gives a more objective view of the situation: 'Dorothy hopes by skilful management to subdue & bring him back . . . Outlook doubtful. Madame is really very completely & devastatingly in love.'[53] Harold Watkins recalls that this was a very difficult time for Edwards: '[s]he walked the hills alone for hours at a stretch, day after day, week after week, working off her "nerves", trying to find calm'.[54]

While Edwards's distress is evident, her letters from this period suggest that she saw Thorburn as a mentor rather than a lover: '[h]e can teach me all the things I want to know at the moment' she wrote in a characteristically lively letter to Jones.[55] The nature of her relationship with her father and his death at such a formative age for Edwards offers a model for her relationship with Thorburn, a figure of authority and guidance, which perpetuates the student–teacher relationship that she shared with her father. This pattern was to be repeated in her relationships with men throughout the rest of her adult life.

Edwards graduated from Cardiff in 1924 with an upper-second-class honours degree. Job opportunities outside university, however, were few. Edwards, like many other university-educated women of her generation, was expected to become a teacher. Given the limited nature of the opportunities open to her perhaps it is hardly surprising that she expressed such distaste when friends and family attempted to persuade her to enter the profession. 'Teaching is very tiring to the temperament', says Antonia Trenier in 'Rhapsody' (*R* 12), a view that Edwards apparently shared with her character. A postgraduate degree was considered, before she declared her ambition to become a full-time writer despite the concerns expressed by her family and friends. 'An author Dorothy wants to be, you know', said Vida to friends and family, perhaps unconvincingly.[56]

'[Vida] would have liked her [Edwards] to take a school-teaching job but the dear little lady seemed somehow to be in awe of Dorothy, and would do nothing that might hinder her from becoming a writer' comments Harold Watkins.[57] Edwards resolutely refused to follow the path so well trodden by her parents and her peers. 'It is absurd to work all day & then try & write in the evening', she wrote to Jones, afraid that teaching would sap the energy that she wished to devote to writing.[58]

Although nominally a student of Greek and philosophy, during her time at university Edwards's love of literature had become increasingly evident. Often to be found in the streets of Cardiff loaded down with 'half-a-dozen novels or plays', she read avidly, particularly European and Russian literature (references to such authors as Hamsun, Selma Lagerlöf, Tolstoy and Dostoevsky abound in her letters to Jones and Kelly).[59] A short story and some topical pieces of her composition had appeared in *Cap and Gown*, and shortly after she had graduated, her short story 'A Country House' appeared in 1925 in Edgell Rickword's influential but short-lived periodical, *The Calendar of Modern Letters*, which he edited with Douglas Garman. A modernist with an eye for talent, Rickword was quick to recognize Edwards's potential, and two further stories of hers, 'The Conquered' and 'Summer-time', appeared in the *Calendar* soon afterwards. In 1926, 'A Country House' was included in Edward J. O'Brien's *Best Short Stories*, alongside work by Aldous Huxley and D. H. Lawrence.[60] Edwards was eager to share her success with her friends, as Watkins recalled:

> One morning she arrived at our house in Rhiwbina bringing us a copy of the . . . magazine 'The Calendar' which contained a short story of hers. She was characteristically modest about it but she knew how pleased we would be and there was no mistaking her sense of elation.[61]

Edwards's own description of her feelings on being published is somewhat understated. 'The Calendar is out & I am on the front page. I suppose that is nice', she wrote in a letter to Beryl Jones on the appearance of 'The Conquered' in April 1926.[62]

Edwards attempted to maintain her connections with the academic and literary quarters of Cardiff and her recent literary success evidently made an impression on her peers. Glyn Jones recalls seeing Edwards at 'some function at the University' where she appeared to him to be 'infinitely more experienced and assured, the last word in chic and sophistication'.[63] She had a similar impact on Gwyn Jones, who 'beheld her with awe' when he saw her in the late 1920s, 'swanning along a College corridor at Cardiff in a broad-brimmed black hat, grass-green costume, the longest ear-rings this side of Tiger Bay, and a cigarette-holder whose fifteen inches of elephant ivory ensured that you got more of the smoke than the smoker'.[64] But with her university studies over and her college friends dispersed, she began to find herself increasingly cut off from the round of lectures and social events that had kept her so engaged during her degree. As Tony Brown notes, many of her literary neighbours like W. J. Gruffydd (at this time professor of Celtic at Cardiff) and his associates were, on the whole, substantially older than Edwards, closer to her mother's generation than to her own.[65]

After graduating, Edwards took up a part-time, temporary job to supplement her mother's pension, and continued to work on her short stories. Life at home, however, became ever more difficult. The responsibility for running the household was increasingly falling on Edwards's shoulders as Vida, who turned sixty in 1926, began to suffer from arthritis. The lack of a secure household income soon became a bone of contention between mother and daughter. Edwards's letters from this period lose their playful tone and instead become characterized by a sense of stifling isolation. 'I am fearfully bored except for Tolstoy & Hugo Wolf & Yasmin. I hardly ever see a soul', she says (Yasmin was her beloved cat).[66] Then, despite the poor financial situation in which she and her mother found themselves after Edward Edwards's death, in May 1926 they let out 9 Pen-y-dre and embarked on a nine-month trip to Europe.[67]

Edwards's love of music and art, her aptitude for languages, a longing to spend some time abroad for the benefit of her literary muse, and perhaps above all the potential of release from everyday distractions, all combined to make the Continent an attractive proposition for the young writer. Vida, perhaps aware of Edwards's loneliness and the aftermath of her relationship with Thorburn ('I find in myself a new & surprising tendency to run three miles away from anyone with whom there is the slightest possibility that I shall fall in love . . . who would have thought that poor John Thorburn could have made such an impression on my soul', Edwards confessed to Beryl Jones) evidently saw the need for a break.[68] But the financial strain that the trip would occasion, not only during their travels but on their return to Cardiff, concerned both mother and daughter. In the approach to their departure, Edwards wrote to Jones:

> [J]udging by the bill we are presently going to receive we shall be going to Vienna in high style. It remains to be seen how we shall come back. When I see how much this venture is going to cost my heart sinks into my slippers and I see a great many advantages in going to seek your fortune with a bundle tied up in a handkerchief.[69]

Edward Edwards's pension and an income from letting out their Cardiff home funded the trip, and although while abroad Edwards was engaged to teach English to a few young pupils by an agency, often such job opportunities were declined due to her commitment to her writing. 'I nearly got a job on Monday, but I refused that . . . on the strength of the *Calendar* wanting another story', she wrote to Jones.[70] Another position as a companion to an Italian lady, which would have taken her to Florence and left her with plenty of time to write, was declined as a result of her chaperoned status. 'I nearly went myself only there is mother', she said.[71]

The pair travelled to Vienna, where they stayed firstly in a flat owned by a retired general, and then on the outskirts of the city in the home of a 'literary woman' who 'knows many Swedish novelists'; Edwards hoped that this connection might 'lead to some translating work later on'.[72] Among their acquaintances were musicians, journalists and publishers, including a Polish violinist with whom Edwards was particularly taken. Edwards soaked up the cultural atmosphere. Her letters from this period are filled with long, vivid descriptions of visits to art galleries, trips to the theatre and to operas. 'I never read!!!' she told Beryl Jones, 'I am dependant [*sic*] for inspiration entirely on concerts.'[73] Already able to read Greek fluently, her German improved quickly and she took Russian lessons. 'I was able to translate everything put before me to my intense surprise. But now that I find that other people besides Dostoievsky [sic] & Turgeniev [sic] etc speak it, it has lost some of its charm', she wrote to Jones.[74]

As Edwards had hoped, her work benefited from her new experiences and her release from domestic worries, and she soon produced several new short stories. 'The Conquered', 'Summer-time', 'A Country House', 'Rhapsody', 'Treachery in a Forest' and 'Cultivated People', which were written in Wales, were soon joined by 'Sweet Grapes', 'A Garland of Earth' and 'Days', which were completed in Vienna.[75] The fact that many of the stories included in *Rhapsody* were either written or amended during Edwards's trip may contribute to their shared holiday motif – almost all of the stories are framed within a visit or holiday of one of the central characters. Her early association with *The Calendar of Modern Letters* proved fruitful, and Edwards was offered a contract with the Calendar Press for a collection of ten short stories.[76]

Now facing a publisher's deadline, Edwards began to rely heavily for help on Jones, who was engaged at the time in working for an Oxford University doctorate.[77] Jones not only agreed to read and criticize Edwards's work, but she was responsible for more mundane, administrative tasks, including making copies of various stories, making any necessary corrections and even putting the stories in the order that Edwards wished, while also maintaining a link with her publisher while Edwards was abroad. Despite this, the volume is not dedicated to Jones but to Edwards's former music teacher, Fred Stibbs. Edwards was well aware of her debt to Jones, but defended her choice thus: '[h]is name is so deliciously surprising. I feel it ought by all the laws of gratitude to go to you & Kelly, but I can't resist it.'[78] Inspired by her success at securing a contract, Edwards's enthusiasm for her writing increased, and in a letter from Vienna she outlines her plans for future projects: 'Next week I shall probably start on the novel. It seems to me that I am improving steadily. Please read my last three stories in the proper order & tell me if that is true. The novel should be much better written.'[79]

But at this apparently fruitful, happy time, there are indications of Edwards's troubled nature and of the unhappiness to come, both in her letters and her work. 'I am not altogether happy here, but it was impossible to stay in Cardiff any longer', she wrote to Jones.[80] Edwards's letters from this period offer the first indication of the depression that would continue to plague her for the rest of her life:

> Everything is very nice here. I go to the opera & I go for wonderful tramps every Sunday with some comparatively nice student, & twice a week I teach a small fat Jewess English, & that only means going for nice walks with her & talking distinctly, & last night I went to a lecture on poison gas & understood at least a quarter of it. I am sunburnt & my voice is getting very strong again and the Polish professor thinks it is good, and there are wonderful films on in the cinemas, even Russian films. And everything is very inspiring & charming. And I am ashamed to say that I am bored & depressed almost to extinction.[81]

More alarming, however, is the fact that Edwards began to articulate self-destructive feelings; in an undated letter from Vienna (*c*.1926), she wrote to Jones:

> I am paralysed with dread when I think of the future. I shall perhaps live another fifty years. I shall write say 10–15 books (& that is too much). That represents at the most 5 to 7 years regular work. That makes 43–45 years of contemplating suicide. And as a whole human nature seems to be constructed so as not to go further than contemplation.[82]

Such comments persist in Edwards's letters to Jones and Kelly and, during the late 1920s and early 1930s, they lose their flippant tone and become increasingly ominous.

The stories that Edwards was writing at this time are characterized by diffident protagonists excluded from a particular world to which they yearn to belong, a pattern that would continue with her 1928 novel, *Winter Sonata*. Miss Wolf in the story 'Cultivated People', for example, is a German expatriate who teaches music and languages. Living in England, she suffers from a sense of homelessness (although she longs for no particular place) and experiences striking moments of despair and isolation:

She was thinking, 'Why am I here? But wherever I were I should feel like this. The world is the same everywhere. One part of it does not belong to me more than another. I go where there are pupils. If I do go home the stones and trees are not likely to know me. It is all the same that I stay here. Oh, my God!' (*R*, 93–4)

Miss Wolf, like Edwards, is adrift, anchorless. *Rhapsody* is full of such poignant and recognizable moments that emphasize the extreme isolation of the characters. In 'Treachery in a Forest', Mr Wendover is left painfully aware of his single status after a brief acquaintance with a holidaying couple. Wendover is spending his annual summer holiday in a dilapidated cottage on the outskirts of a forest. While walking one day he meets Leo and Elizabeth Harding, and during the following few days Wendover builds up their brief acquaintance into something quite significant. He visits their cottage one evening, carrying carefully three eggs as a gift. '[W]hy did you bring three instead of two?' asks Elizabeth, emphasizing Wendover's exclusion from them as a couple (*R*, 68). There is no hiding his dismay when they inform him that their holiday ends shortly, and he prepares himself for their final meeting by 'walking as far as the place where he had first met them, as though to revise the first stages in their acquaintance' (*R*, 76). He returns from this walk to a note informing him that they have had to depart earlier than planned, and that their farewell gathering can no longer take place. His heart sinks, he feels 'acutely disappointed' and suddenly realizes the 'fatal significance' of the packing case that stood outside their cottage (*R*, 76, 77). He writes a response to Elizabeth, thanking them for their company and regretting its loss (he has only known them for three days), but does not post it: 'On the way back to the house he began to feel depressed, and before he reached there he tore up the letter and did not send it after all' (*R*, 77). *Rhapsody*, like Edwards's letters from this period, leaves the reader with a sense of the soul-destroying isolation of the individual, and the inability of people to make meaningful contact with one another.

After brief but expensive stays in Florence and Venice en route from Austria, Edwards and Vida returned to Cardiff to be greeted with the proofs of *Rhapsody*. 'I am very pleased with the publishers.

Even the outside paper cover is nice. It is green & blue & very long & you know green & blue is my favourite combination of colours', she wrote to Jones.[83] '[*Rhapsody*] cries out for some companion volumes, so I am endeavouring to write one', she commented in a further letter.[84] Her trip had left her 'fuller of projects than of anything else – for an essay on [Vasily Vasilievich] Rozanov, a monograph on Hugo Wolf'.[85] Her appetite for travel whetted, and her mother appeased by her literary success, Edwards at once planned future trips, this time alone:

> I intend spending next winter in Paris. Mother stays here. It depends of course on money. But I am so anxious to do it as a preliminary to persuading mother that I shall not be crucified upside down if I go to Moscow in the following year. In Paris I expect to be depressed, but I long for Moscow. Venice brought back all my old enthusiasm probably.[86]

But Edwards's plans to travel alone were soon put on hold. Vida was becoming increasingly dependent on her daughter and Edwards soon found it difficult to get away, even for short periods. As the influence of her European trip faded, her return to familiar surroundings and the demands and distractions of everyday life soon made the task of finishing the novel that she had begun writing while in Europe, about which she had written to Jones so excitedly, difficult. In a letter to Kelly she wrote:

> I am fearfully stuck in the mud with my novel [*Winter Sonata*]. I ought to have a den . . . & go into it & lock the door & not come out until I had produced one. Only it is too reminiscent of the immaculate conception to suit my temperament.[87]

Winter Sonata remained unfinished until Edwards managed to escape from Cardiff for a short period to stay with Jones who, by this point, had given up her studies at Oxford and had taken up a teaching post in Yorkshire, where she was soon joined by Kelly. 'I should most certainly never have finished the novel – if I had not finished it there', she wrote to Jones.[88] The novel's writing had been interrupted by a request from Edgell Rickword for Edwards to contribute an essay on G. K. Chesterton to his *Scrutinies* collection, which appeared in

1928. With the completion of *Winter Sonata*, Edwards established a pattern: she was apparently unable to sustain or complete her creative work at home in Cardiff.

2

Narrating males/muted females: silence and song in *Rhapsody*

'A Country House' was the first story that Edwards attempted to publish.[1] It is also one of the best examples of her unique literary technique. The story is narrated from the perspective of a middle-aged country gentleman who, addressing an implied sympathetic audience, inadvertently reveals his tyrannical nature and sense of ownership over his young wife. The couple live in an isolated country manor; on a whim, the owner decides that he would like to have it supplied with electricity, and becomes increasingly jealous of his wife's relationship with the electrician hired to carry out the job. As the installation progresses, so the increasing irrationality in the narrator's behaviour towards his wife is revealed. Edwards underlines the narrator's role as possessor throughout: he is never named, so the reader has little choice but to categorize him as 'the owner', and the fact that he neglects to give his wife's name emphasizes his view of her as lacking an integral self, being, in effect, his property.

Edwards's owner is at once a comic and sinister figure as he continually, and unconvincingly, tries to justify his actions to his audience. His assumption of shared values with his implied reader adds to the effect of his irrationality and he becomes increasingly defensive. While spying on his wife and the electrician he justifies his actions to the reader, revealing a sense of guilt, or perhaps impropriety:

> They stood up, and I waited for them to come through the door. *I suppose nobody could expect me to hide behind a tree so as to cause them no embarrassment* . . . However, they chose to go back by the other way along the bank of the stream. (*R*, 41; my emphasis)

Throughout 'A Country House' the owner continually attempts to control and oppress his wife, fearing that if she is left to her own devices she will become completely wild and uninhibited. While the wife is associated with the natural world throughout, her husband, in his desire for electricity and his association with the technological, seems to represent a sort of false, unnatural existence. From the day of their marriage, when she has to tie back her long, curly hair, her husband denies her anything natural that pleases her. His destruction of a wild part of the garden in which she takes particular pleasure is indicative of his controlling and vindictive nature:

> When we got to the bottom of the garden and through the door which opens on the bank of the stream she gave a cry of horror. And I will tell you why. It was because I had had the grass and weeds on the bank cut.
> She turned to Richardson. 'I am so sorry,' she said. 'You should have seen this before it was cut. It was very pretty. What were those white flowers growing on the other side?'
> 'Hemlock,' I said. 'It had to be cut.'
> 'I don't see why,' she said. 'It is a pity to spoil such a beautiful place for the sake of tidiness.' She turned to him petulantly.
> Now that is all nonsense. A place must be tidy. There were bulrushes and water-lilies as it was. What more must she have? A lot of weeds dripping down into the water! There is a difference between garden flowers and weeds. If you want weeds, then do not have gardens. And I suppose I am insensible to beauty because I keep the place cut and trimmed. Nonsense! Suppose my wife took off her clothes and ran about the garden like a bacchante! Perhaps I should like it very much, but I should shut her up in her room all the same. (R, 34–5)

Like the abandoned and uninhibited followers of Bacchus, the 'bringer of ecstasy and of wine', the owner's wife is a force of disorder that must be controlled by his male rationality and locked up if she transgresses, just as his electric generator will undermine the natural order of day and night.

The owner, then, is fearful of his wife's sexuality and its potential expression. Music is imagined as its medium and, as a result, the husband considers his wife's choice of song to play to the electrician inappropriate:

She played a Chopin nocturne. Now I could watch girls dancing to Chopin's music all day, but to play Chopin to a stranger that you meet for the first time! What must he think of you? I can understand her playing even the nocturnes when she is alone. When one is alone one is in the mood for anything. But to choose to play them when she is meeting someone for the first time! That is simply wrong. (*R*, 32)

By playing Chopin for Richardson, then, the owner's wife, as the owner sees it, has expressed the sexuality that he fears and oppresses.

Such a male narrative voice is characteristic of *Rhapsody*. Of the ten stories included in the volume, four make use of a first-person male narrator who is also a central character ('Rhapsody', 'A Country House', 'The Conquered' and 'A Garland of Earth'). The remaining six are told by an unnamed narrator to whom we are never introduced, as is 'La Penseuse', a story that Edwards originally intended for inclusion in *Rhapsody*, but which she cut. But even when the narrators are unnamed or unspecified, on the whole they are nonetheless implicitly male. 'Sweet Grapes', for example, opens with the line, 'My friend Hugo Ferris decided, a few summers ago, to taste to the full the pleasures of solitude' (*R*, 111). While this may not be enough to allow us to identify the narrator as definitively male, the attitudes and observations subtly put forward throughout the narrative are. When Elizabeth, the young female occupant of the house in which Ferris is spending his holiday, asks if she may borrow the book that he is reading when he has finished with it, the narrator's response is typical of Edwards's male narrators: 'It was a book on the eighteenth-century Enlightenment, and hardly likely to interest a girl of nineteen', he says (*R*, 114; such a book would, of course, have interested a 19-year-old Edwards).

The pompous middle-class male is a signature character for Edwards. The deliberate manner in which such misogyny is revealed in stories such as 'A Country House' and 'Sweet Grapes' leaves the reader with a lasting sense of the inequity of sexual and social hierarchies. The intensity of the short story form is particularly amenable to this technique: Edwards's manipulation of the male first-person narrative may have proved more difficult to sustain in a longer form. Critical theory on the short story and gender suggests that the form may offer ideological as much as aesthetic appeal. Clare Hanson has argued that 'the short story has been from its inception a particularly appropriate vehicle for the expression of the ex-centric, alienated vision of women':

> The short story has offered itself to losers and loners, exiles, women, blacks – writers who for one reason or another have not been part of the ruling 'narrative' or epistemological/experiential framework of their society.[2]

Doubly marginalized as a woman and as a Welsh writer, debarred both from the patriarchal leisured society that she chose to depict and the male-dominated working-class society from which she came, the short story became Edwards's chosen vehicle.

The adoption by female writers of a male narrative voice to expose, undermine and mock patriarchy has not historically been recognized as a feminist technique. In her essay on May Sinclair's 1904 novel *The Divine Fire*, Diana Wallace argues that the author's choice of a male protagonist has in fact led to its neglect by those who played key roles in reclaiming Sinclair's other works. Wallace suggests that feminist critics 'have tended until very recently to focus on writers' depictions of women as a way of exploring the construction and problematics of femininity'.[3] Of late, however, feminist criticism has acknowledged the complex and subversive nature of such narrative mimicry and its implications for understanding women's writing.

Edwards was not the first Welsh woman writing in English to whom this technique appealed. Nineteenth-century industrialist and feminist activist Amy Dillwyn adopts a male, working-class voice in her 1880 novel *The Rebecca Rioter* to mock the misguided philanthropy and perceived superiority of her own wealthy social group. Dillwyn based her novel on a passage written by her father, Lewis Llewelyn Dillwyn, a Swansea Liberal MP and member of the nouveau riche, which recorded his encounter with the working-class men who, disguised in women's clothing and operating under the collective 'Daughters of Rebecca', attacked turnpikes throughout

Wales as a protest to the exorbitant fees levied for their use. In her introduction to the text, Katie Gramich argues:

> *The Rebecca Rioter* is an unusual novel for an avowed feminist to have written, adopting a male protagonist and a male voice. However, through her male mouthpiece . . . Dillwyn questions some of the cherished truths of her society and invites the reader to join her in that questioning and ultimately subversive attitude.[4]

Far from prioritizing a male perspective, then, writers like Edwards question the very nature of patriarchy and the power relations inherent in their society. Judith Butler has argued that cross-dressing 'implicitly suggests that gender is a kind of impersonation that passes as the real . . . [it] destabilizes the very distinctions between the natural and the artificial, depth and surface, inner and outer through which discourse about genders almost always operates'.[5] Butler is writing here of men in drag, dressing and posing as women, but this argument is equally valid in terms of women posing as men, and has significant, though different, implications in terms of social commentary for the understanding of Edwards and other writers who choose to mimic a male voice. As Wallace suggests, the key issue in female writers using the male voice is power politics: 'a cross-dressing [or cross-writing] woman is masking her *lack* of power', it 'does not silence the male but exposes masculinity as constructed and contingent, thus undermining its traditionally universalized and normative status'.[6] By deconstructing the primacy of the male through her use of the narrative voice and revealing 'what was supposed to remain invisible' in her society through questioning the cultural superiority it endowed upon the male, Edwards questions the validity of hegemonic standards.[7]

The narrator of 'A Country House' would find a kindred spirit in Hugo Ferris in 'Sweet Grapes'. Ostensibly seeking peace and solitude, he has rented a section of a mock castle in the Peak District for his holiday. The building's only other occupants are its house-keeper, Mrs Lester, and her 19-year-old cousin, Elizabeth. The story is narrated by a friend of Ferris who appears to consider himself kindly disposed to the plight of such isolated and vulnerable young women as Elizabeth, but his speculations on her feelings, coupled with the fact that he continually claims to share Ferris's outlook, reveal a poisonous attitude.

Elizabeth and Ferris spend some time together and share, on occasion, a kiss (Ferris considers this an annoying indulgence to Elizabeth and rather a chore on his part). Both Ferris and the narrator assume that Elizabeth has been dreaming of the advent into her life of a man like Ferris:

> it is a great embarrassment when a young girl has lived so much alone without friends and has dreamed about the future and about love and all that sort of thing, and has made, as it were, a whole world of her own; and then suddenly someone who is not only a dream but also a fact comes into this world, and immediately this fact seems to her to fit exactly into the framework she has made, or if it does not fit, she forces it to do so, and stands weeping and breaking her heart because she can neither give up the dreams nor the reality. (R, 113–14)

Elizabeth's simple request that Ferris should recommend to her some contemporary authors results in a response derogatory not only to her intellectual capabilities (he initially recommends Aldous Huxley but withdraws the comment as 'she would not understand the conversations', R, 115) but to women in general ('he knew that most women only talk about reading, and this is merely the preliminary to talking about love', R, 115). The narrator, despite his continual proclamations that he does 'see Ferris' point of view', appears to demonstrate a more kindly attitude towards Elizabeth, but he also discloses, without seeming to recognize that he does so, his own predatory attitude towards young women like her and his envy of his friend for what he was apparently offered. He says:

> And of course I quite understand that his relationship with Elizabeth did not provide any suitable conversation. And yet one would think that a young girl growing up there, with her soul opening out, so to speak, hanging on the lowest bough waiting to be plucked and all that sort of thing, would be rather nice. (R, 123)

27

Ferris endeavours to treat Elizabeth as if she is undeserving of the courtesy and respect that he, as a cultured and intelligent man, would show his fellow (presumably male) human beings. He depicts Elizabeth to his narrator friend as a dim-witted, overly emotional, sentimental girl – in short a typical woman in Ferris's eyes – with nothing of value to give to the world, in contrast to his perception of himself as an intelligent, cultured and altogether superior being. And yet, in 'Sweet Grapes' the narrator reveals that Ferris did not find his holiday, nor Elizabeth, as dull as he claims. Through disclosing how much he had been told of the intricacies of Ferris's stay, the amount of time that he spent with Elizabeth, and her beauty and grace (to which Ferris claimed to have been impervious), the narrator reveals that Elizabeth had personality and presence enough to make her, in fact, difficult to forget. But the most haunting image of the tale is the 'Sleeping Beauty' aspect of its portrayal of women as forced to wait in passivity for the advent of their 'prince', with no opportunity to create a life of their own.

This theme recurs throughout *Rhapsody*. In 'Summer-time', Joseph Laurel has been invited to accompany his tennis partner, Beatrice Hammond, on a trip to stay with her sister, Mrs Chalen, at her home in the country. At the house are Beatrice's teenage niece, Leonora, and the girl's cousin, Basil; both are just out of school, and are filled with youthful exuberance. As the holiday progresses, Laurel associates himself increasingly with the two young cousins rather than with his contemporary, Beatrice: 'The curious thing is that he does not remember noticing Beatrice much during all this time . . . so completely had he given himself up to the atmosphere of the country and the garden and the roses, and Leonora with them' (*R*, 104). Laurel demonstrates a childlike, and somewhat irritating, naivety in his relations with Leonora, executed with comic precision and encapsulated in a conversation between the two about school: 'he thought what a large gulf there was between them . . . Not, you know, that he was nearly forty and she seventeen, but merely that he had left school a term before her' (*R*, 106). Unable to comprehend the warnings conveyed in Beatrice's 'little smile[s] of malice and veiled amusement' (*R*, 104), Laurel continues to perceive Leonora and Basil as his peers, looking increasingly foolish in the process. When the party return home from a picnic,

> Basil began to sing, beating time with a dusty branch in his hand, and Leonora joined in. Mr Laurel did not know the song, but he joined in too, singing anything to the tune. And again he caught Beatrice looking at him with a malicious little smile, which he resented without quite knowing why. (R, 106)

The following day, Laurel is forced to realize the impossibility of his relations with the young cousins when, unobserved, he watches Basil and Leonora in the garden:

> [Basil] bent down, put his arms round her shoulders, and kissed her, on the cheek though, not on her mouth.
> . . . Basil laughed, and felt, I dare say, awfully wicked and daring. But he was a little embarrassed too. For lack of anything to say he kissed her again, and she hid her face against his macintosh. They sat down side by side, and could not even look at each other. Then Basil said something with a casual air, nonchalantly turned a cartwheel somersault on the wet grass, and they walked out through the gate, looking straight ahead of them, and with the mark of the brown turfs across the backs of their macintoshes.
> And as they passed out of the gate it seemed to Mr Laurel that his youth vanished with them . . . He felt an overwhelming melancholy within his soul, and yet it seemed, too, as if he were on the threshold of a thought that would console him, when, looking up, he saw Beatrice sitting reading just outside the house. She was in white again, ready to play [tennis] when the grass was dry. He suddenly began to see why she had smiled with such malice. It was at the spectacle of him fatuously running after a schoolgirl, anxiously watching each little blush, as though blushes were not simply a physical characteristic of schoolgirls. He nearly blushed himself at the thought. It would have been far more appropriate if he had carried on a flirtation with Beatrice, who was nearer his own age. He suddenly felt even more alarmed. He recalled the number of times he had played tennis with Beatrice and taken her out, without ever having considered that she was of a marriageable age. But now that he had discovered that he was himself middle-aged, he began to see that he had behaved in a most compromising manner. He almost ran across the lawn, intending in a few moments' conversation to efface his unconscious behaviour of years. But he stumbled up the

steps, and when he got to her he felt a little embarrassed, perhaps not unnaturally.

Beatrice looked slowly up from her book as though she believed he had come especially to tell her something. This put what he had meant to say out of his head, and after a moment's embarrassing silence he hurriedly looked down the garden and said, 'It will soon be dry enough for tennis.' (R, 107–9)

This is a prime example of Edwards's technique and, as such, is worth quoting at length. Laurel's realization is both vehement and visually effective: we can see the confusion and panic in his face as he recognizes the implications of his actions, follow him as he mounts the steps and stumbles, and watch as his courage leaves him when confronted with the formidable Beatrice – the implications of her white attire now all too clear to the shell-shocked Laurel. And yet this comic scene is also filled with pathos: the 'overwhelming melancholy within his soul' that Laurel feels when he realizes his separation from Basil and Leonora, and his 'discovery' that he 'was himself middle-aged' highlight the fleeting nature of human existence. Most of all, we are left with a sense of the inability of individuals to connect in a meaningful manner, a theme that dominates Edwards's work and, ultimately, her outlook on life. Unable to face travelling back to town with Beatrice, Laurel makes an excuse to end his holiday early and, rather than acknowledge and apologize for his behaviour towards her, he goes to extreme lengths to avoid her: 'Now he has decided to go abroad for the winter because he finds that his diary is full of engagements with Beatrice, and he is only waiting to keep some quite inevitable ones . . . and then he will escape' (R, 110).

Laurel's experience is characteristic of *Rhapsody*; Edwards's characters rapidly approach their moment of realization only to fail to seize the opportunity for change, or to miss their epiphany altogether. The nature of Laurel's realization is ambiguous: is he sorry for the inconsiderate manner in which he has treated his friend Beatrice? Is he embarrassed about the impropriety of his actions or desolate about the passing of his youth? 'People do not change their lives suddenly. That is, they don't except in literature', says Richardson in 'A Country House' (*R*, 40). In *Rhapsody*, the moment of epiphany is not a stimulus for change in Edwards's characters, but rather serves to reinforce the static nature of their lives. The reader sees that the character has reached a crisis point, an opportunity for self-realization and change; the character, however, wavers on the brink but then withdraws quickly, refusing to acknowledge the potential for revelation and continuing to live in the same way with the same (seemingly obvious) problems. In *Rhapsody*, more often than not, the significance of the epiphany or revelation has completely passed the experiencing character by.

In 'Summer-time', the contrast between the plans of the two young people, Basil and Leonora, serves to emphasize the lack of opportunity, or choice, open to young women. Basil has decided to be a dancer but Leonora appears to have no particular ambition. Her mother, Mrs Chalen, asks Mr Laurel's advice on Leonora's future:

> [Mrs Chalen] 'I don't know what to let her do.'
> 'Has she any particular talents?' he asked.
> 'None that I know anything about,' said her mother, looking at Leonora severely . . .
> 'I think she should go to an art school,' he [Laurel] said to her mother.
> 'Do you really think so?' said she. 'Can you paint, dear?'
> 'I don't know,' said Leonora.
> 'Oh, that doesn't matter' said Mr Laurel, smiling at her. 'Some artist will marry her because he wants to paint her hair, and they will live happily ever afterwards.'
> 'Yes,' said Leonora, with innocent approval.
> 'You really think so?' said her mother, smiling a little doubtfully.
> 'Undoubtedly,' said Mr Laurel.
> And thus her fate was decided, for sure enough she has gone to an art school. (*R*, 99)

Laurel's suggestion that Leonora should attend an art school in order to find a husband rather than embark upon a creative journey of her own is apparently meant kindly, but the socially regressive tone of the comment is clear. Laurel's humiliation at the end of the story on his sudden and fleeting realization of the inappropriate nature of his behaviour towards the various women he has encountered is presented as just punishment for all his ignorant assumptions about their sex. Equally, though, Mrs Chalen's quandary here about her daughter's future is very telling – she is at odds about what to 'let' Leonora do. Such a verb would not be used in relation to a son. While Leonora waits for someone to tell her what she is to do in life, Basil has made a very definite decision as to his own future career path, and appears to have reached this conclusion without any outside interference or advice.

Most of the young women in *Rhapsody* are equally as apathetic about their future careers as Leonora. In 'A Throne in Heaven', the pre-pubescent orphan Sidney Mihail is a budding poet sensitive to the natural world around him, who spends his holidays reading Rossetti and writing poetry in the boarding school of which he is a pupil. Sidney is invited by Mr Merill, an old friend of his father, to spend the holiday at the Merill family home. Merill's daughter, Elizabeth, who is of a similar age to Sidney, suffers from an un-specified illness which necessitates much rest and little excitement. Apart from a pale countenance, however, Elizabeth appears to be equally robust as Sidney ('They make an awful fuss over me. It is all nonsense', Elizabeth tells Sidney: *R*, 142). The pair spend their time playing, reading and writing in a nearby pine forest, where Sidney reveals his poetic aspirations. 'I expect I shall get married', says Elizabeth, when Sidney enquires as to her ambitions (*R*, 145).

The process of socialization, of absorbing the norms and expect-ations of society, has already begun to influence Elizabeth's perception of the world and her place in it. Sidney, however, remains impervious: he makes Elizabeth a thyrsus, for example, because he has read of one in Swinburne, but is unaware of its connotations of sexual excess.[8] As yet gender and class conditioning have not fully permeated Elizabeth's consciousness, and the pair are able to enjoy an equal and innocent relationship as a result of their ignorance of social, and indeed sexual, conventions. The 'Throne in Heaven' of the title is the pre-socialized world that the children inhabit when they are alone, free from the civic rules and conventions that will all too soon come to dominate their lives in adulthood.

Edwards's preoccupation with the lack of choices open to young women seems to have its roots in her own experiences. As I have suggested, her refusal to take up a teaching career signalled a stance against the limited world of employment available to educated young women in patriarchal society. In 'La Penseuse', the most overtly autobiographical of Edwards's stories, a stark contrast is drawn between the opportunities available to young women compared with their male counterparts and the devastating impact this can have. Written in 1925–6, it is one of her earliest stories, and the only one composed and then rejected for inclusion in *Rhapsody*.[9] Although some similarities exist between this tale and those finally published in *Rhapsody* (a foreboding sense of isolation, for example, permeates 'La Penseuse' as much as the other stories), it does sit uncomfortably with the volume as a whole. Its characters are the lower- and middle-class inhabitants of a small village, rather than the upper-middle classes that populate Edwards's other stories. Edwards was evidently aware of the discrepancies in its theme and focus: commenting on the collection as a whole, she told Jones, 'In all the stories the uncommon people are most important & the commonplace ones less so. In "La Penseuse" the commonplace people are more important. Now that's very clever, but of course quite dull.'[10]

Although narrated from an assumed male perspective, in this story Edwards's focus rests more completely than elsewhere on a female character. Mary, the female thinker of the title, is a young woman 'possessed by a perfect fever for acquiring knowledge' who lives in near poverty with her elderly and invalid aunt on the outskirts of an unnamed village (*R*, 198).[11] The similarity between her character's circumstances and Edwards's own, living alone with her elderly mother in near poverty on the outskirts of Cardiff, are evident. Mary's only pleasure comes from her friendship with two local young men, Sidney Mertris and Richard Warnham, both of whom are at college. Intelligent and quick to learn, Mary 'considered wasted every moment she spent with them in which they did not impart to her something interesting and instructive' (*R*, 198–9). On their part, both Sidney and Richard do their best to teach her:

> Sidney taught her a fair amount of anatomy with success, and there was nothing in philosophy, if Richard could explain it to her in language that was not technical, which she did not understand, though he had not at that time read very much on the subject himself. (*R*, 199)

Both men leave the area once their careers take off and Mary is left to care for her aunt. Some fifteen years later, following her aunt's death, Mary spends some time travelling in Europe as a lady's companion before returning to Britain and finding herself, coincidentally, employed as Sidney's housekeeper. The pair immediately fall back into their teacher-pupil roles: now a respected surgeon, Sidney proceeds to educate Mary in the intricacies of various operations while she, once her limited housekeeping duties are over, spends her time poring over the books in his library. Here she finds, alongside Sidney's extensive *oeuvre* of medical books, 'essays on art and architecture and on travel' by their old friend Richard (*R*, 207). Mary acts more as Sidney's literary assistant than his housekeeper: she is privy to his conversations with his medical friends, 'listening avidly to everything they let fall', and helps him with a book that he is writing (*R*, 208). But although Mary soon 'knew exactly how to perform many delicate and difficult operations' (*R*, 213), she is merely a guest in the male intellectual realm, and Edwards draws a sharp contrast between the domestic and the intellectual spheres: 'Sidney, as he finished each page of his book, read it to her or handed it to her to be read. Much of it she copied out in the handwriting with which she wrote the dates on the covers of jampots' (*R*, 207).

With Mary's help, Sidney's book is soon finished. While Mary continues to absorb herself in the library, Sidney spends his evenings out in town and soon becomes engaged 'to the daughter of one of the richest surgeons in England' (*R*, 213). The match is driven by Sidney's ambition rather than any love or even affection for his future bride: 'Really I am very lucky. She is young and beautiful and very distinguished and it is a good match in every way', he says to Mary (*R*, 213). Sidney's fiancée and her father visit the house for dinner and while Sidney admires his bride's 'expensive clothes', his future father-in-law 'lighted in astonishment on Mary's knowledge of surgery' (R, 214).

Sidney is married and Mary, once again redundant, returns to the village of her birthplace. Having given up her life to the pursuit of knowledge, she has nothing to show for it, whereas Sidney has a successful career, a practice and now a wife, and Richard too has his substantial list of publications. But this is no tragic love story: there is not a sense of a relationship or romance lost, but of a life wasted. Mary has largely been a passive receptor which both Richard and (especially) Sidney have been able to use to work out their own ideas, theories and plans for their futures, and then discarded. The story ends with a scene that epitomizes both female passivity and the contrast between the opportunities available to women as opposed to men as Mary, lonely and unfulfilled, 'sat before the fire and began to think about her life' (R, 215).

Not all of Edwards's female characters are as passive as Elizabeth in 'A Throne in Heaven' or Leonora in 'Summer-time' when it comes to determining their life occupations, yet they still find themselves victims of circumstance or social expectations. The central female character in 'A Garland of Earth' is 17-year-old Rahel, a scientific 'genius' whose mental capability is admired by the men in her household: her father, Mr Coleman, her 11-year-old brother, Jimmy, and her father's laboratory assistant, Mr Froud (R, 132). Edwards gave some clue to the type of character that she was trying to create in Rahel in a letter to Beryl Jones. She wrote of 'A Garland of Earth': 'The girl in it I got from a newspaper – & therefore probably quite inaccurate, picture of the daughter of Madam Curie, who was aged 16 & already a Ph.D or something.'[12]

The family is visited by the elderly Mr Leonard, the story's narrator, at their isolated home near the coast (Rahel suffers from an unspecified complaint which necessitates exposure to sea air). In preparation for his visit, Leonard purchases gifts for Coleman's children: a fan for Rahel and a book by Herman Melville for Jimmy. Rahel's unfeminine reaction when given the gift, though she is suitably grateful, disappoints Leonard: 'But she put the little fan into her pocket. She did not hold it up to her face before the mirror', he says despondently (R 128–9). Rahel's comment – 'Nobody has ever given me a present like this before' (R, 128) – is ambiguous: is she touched by the kind gesture or offended by its gendered and superficial nature? Her pre-pubescent brother has, of course, been given a weighty classic.

Leonard is clearly perturbed by the fact that Rahel does not react to his gift in what he considers to be a feminine manner. Much of the comedy, and indeed the criticism, in this story come from Leonard's attitude towards Rahel: despite his conscious attempts to be modern-minded, he continually makes ignorant and derogatory remarks. He recalls one occasion when, during one of their regular walks, he inadvertently offended Rahel:

> Rahel always carried a tin specimen-case with her and collected botanical specimens, and she said that she was making a map of the flora of the district. I remember when she first told me about this, and I said, 'Ah, yes, of course, pressing flowers.'
> She looked at me in surprise, and with perhaps a little impatience. But I had meant only that she was the modern equivalent of the young ladies of another generation who pressed flowers. I am no opponent of the higher education for women. (R, 130)

No matter how hard he tries he cannot help but revert to his trad-itional and outmoded views, despite his protests to the contrary. 'She likes me, but she cannot answer me because she thinks that I do not believe in the higher education for women. Ah, what barriers the young build around themselves!', he thinks after one conversation, unable to see that it is his own views, not Rahel's, that create a barrier between them (R, 134).

The comic effect created by this bumbling but well-intentioned old man is as impressive in its craftsmanship as it is subtle yet effective in its indictment of accepted patriarchal standards. And yet this character voices one of the most moving and suggestive interior monologues in Edwards's *oeuvre*. Leonard, after a walk with the children and Mr Froud, dozes in his armchair after being drenched in a sudden thunderstorm. His last waking thought is this:

I have had a long and a pleasant life. But how can I know what will come before it is over? These few years that I have yet to live will bring something as new and strange to me as anything these children have before them to see. One comes, an old blind man, like old Oedipus at Colonos, leaning on the arm of a girl, looking down with blind eyes on the earth, and suddenly one sees little pink flowers, like children looking up to the sky. One may not rest yet, one may not rest yet. (*R*, 138)

In Sophocles' play Oedipus, elderly and sightless, is led by his daughter Antigone (who in the subsequent play in the series goes on to make a stand against patriarchy) into Colonos, where Oedipus is suddenly able to see the 'little pink flowers' (in Edwards's story representative, perhaps, of women), to which he has previously been blind. In Edwards's story the thunderstorm that soaked the group during their walk, which has perhaps prompted Leonard's realization, is likened to the wrath of the Erinyes, the fearful mythical sisters who avenged wrongs and punished those who transgressed natural boundaries or social laws, especially those associated with matriarchal law:

gradually from the other side of the bay there came a great black cloud. It rose up slowly, gathering strength as it came, and, like one of the Erinyes, stretched its grey hands above us and called to its sisters to follow, as if it brought to one of us the vengeance for some blood-guiltiness . . . (*R*, 136)

I suggest that Leonard, in his semi-conscious musing, acknowledges the transient and fluctuating nature not only of life, but of the laws and proprieties that govern society which had earlier led him to the conclusion that Rahel's scientific experiments extend only to pressing flowers.

All of Edwards's females, then, are in some way oppressed or voiceless, marginalized by illness or age and overpowered by domineering men, or by the shared conventions and boundaries of the society in which they live. In *Rhapsody*, music is the only form of expression that is specifically and consistently linked to women and yet, as musical ability is seen as a desirable attribute in women by many of Edwards's male characters, it is at times a tool complicit in female subjugation. In the title story, 'Rhapsody', music has become an obsession for the central character, George Everett. Mr Elliott, an expatriate visiting London for his annual holiday, meets Everett in a London cafe, where it emerges that Everett is on a rare excursion to a concert. 'I never have the opportunity to hear very much [music] now . . . My wife is an invalid, so that I do not like to leave her for very long', he explains (R, 3). Mrs Everett, once an accomplished pianist, is now housebound due to an unspecified illness and can no longer play her instrument. The discussion that follows convinces Everett that he has found in Elliott a kindred spirit, and he invites him to stay at the family home. Elliott, feeling rather isolated in London, readily accepts.

During Elliott's stay, it becomes clear that Everett's pursuit of music has become a source of tension between him and his wife:

> It was curious how, whenever Everett mentioned music, he looked at her a little apprehensively, and she almost imperceptibly frowned. I wonder if she had awakened one day to find that he had married her because she was a beautiful pianist, and perhaps she took a dislike to music from that day? (R, 6)

Elliott's observation about Everett's motivation in selecting his wife appears to be justified. It emerges that Everett has always relied on the women around him to provide him with music. He says to Elliot, who narrates the story: 'When I was a boy I had a sister who played everything for me, and then my wife was a beautiful pianist, so I never practised myself' (R, 4). Rather than learn himself now that his wife is no longer able to play, Everett instead hatches a deceptive plan to satisfy his thirst for music. Under the guise of providing a governess for his young son, Vincent, who is due to leave for boarding school in two months' time, Everett advertises for a music teacher with knowledge of general subjects.

The covert manner in which Everett arranges for the appointment of a governess indicates that he is, on some level, aware of the inappropriate nature of his actions. He asks Elliot to ensure that Mrs Everett is otherwise occupied when the interviewee, Antonia Trenier, arrives, saying: 'Though there is no harm at all in what I am doing, I should so much prefer it if my wife were not present at the interview' (R, 9). Similarly, the manner in which Everett approaches music at other points in the text suggests that he associates private, secret feelings with its practice, as Elliot discovers on the first evening of his visit:

> After dinner that evening he led me solemnly into the drawing-room. In spite of his passion for music the room had a desolate, unoccupied air, and the music was arranged too neatly. He shut the door very carefully and drew a heavy curtain across it. (R, 9)

Elliott proceeds to sing for his host, but the manner in which this takes place is strange and uncomfortable: 'he made me sing until I was hoarse', he says (R, 9).

The family, accompanied by Elliot and the newly appointed Antonia, visit Scotland for a holiday where, now master of a singer, a pianist and in the landlord of the cottage a violinist, Everett's obsession becomes all-consuming. Elliott says of the trio:

> We obeyed Everett like slaves, even to the extent of playing or singing a single phrase a dozen times over, while he, standing on his toes in the middle of the carpet, strung up to a pitch of the most rapturous torment, would drink in the essence of every note. (R, 14)

Antonia's musical ability makes her an object of attraction for Everett and, following the discovery that she has kept hidden her beautiful singing voice due to a lack of confidence, he no longer conceals his interest in her as a replacement wife. Elliott, apparently able to recognize Everett's selfish behaviour, nonetheless remains silent: he is unwilling to confront Everett and criticize his actions. Instead, he steps quietly but firmly into a guardian role for Vincent and provides companionship to Mrs Everett, whose health rapidly declines. By the end of the holiday Vincent is packed off to boarding school and Mrs Everett, lonely and neglected, dies. Her husband, absorbed in his obsession and his new-found love for Antonia, demonstrates the same disregard and detachment on his wife's death as he did during her illness.

Elliott, Everett and Antonia depart from their holiday in the same train as Mrs Everett's body; Elliott to return to his job in Egypt and Everett to his home, presumably to arrange his wife's burial before marrying Antonia. But there is no suggestion of new life in the relationship between Everett and Antonia; on the contrary, the overriding feeling is that Antonia will suffer the same fate as her predecessor, sapped of her strength and relegated to the parlour once Everett has sucked all her energy from her with his constant demands on her to perform. The rhapsody of the title, it seems, is for Everett alone.

Rather than straightforwardly offering a creative outlet to women, then, female musical performance becomes in *Rhapsody* a mode of display for male enjoyment – another level of oppression. In stories such as 'A Country House', 'Rhapsody' and 'Treachery in a Forest', women are used to channel music for the male voyeur or connoisseur, while here and elsewhere musical performance is read by men as expressive of a sexuality of which the women appear unaware. In 'A Country House', the owner considers his wife's choice of music for their guest to be sexually inappropriate. Likewise, in 'Treachery in a Forest', Mr Harding becomes increasingly antagonistic and jealous as his companion Elizabeth and their acquaintance Mr Wendover explore their shared passion for music, and particularly so after Wendover and Elizabeth play a piano duet together. In 'Cultivated People', set in a music club in an unspecified town, two middle-aged men compete over a musically talented female contemporary. On first appearance, there is little to suggest that Miss Wolf will be such a desired figure: a middle-aged German expatriate who teaches languages, piano and violin, she has 'a rather fat, pale face, and small, very sad brown eyes' (*R*, 80). President of the music club and self-important bachelor Mr Challis attempts to propose marriage to Miss Wolf during a reception at their club, only to be continually and deliberately interrupted by his married friend Mr Gallon, who also apparently desires Miss Wolf as a result of her musical prowess.

In her work on contemporary female performance, Susan McClary suggests that '[w]omen on the stage are viewed as sexual commodities regardless of their appearance or seriousness':[13]

women's bodies in Western culture have almost always been viewed as
objects of display . . . Centuries of this traditional sexual division of labor
. . . [threaten] to convert her [the female performer] . . . once again into
yet another body set in motion for the pleasure of the masculine gaze.[14]

Exhibitionism is not the intention of Edwards's female performers.
Instead, by filtering such observations through a male narrative
voice, Edwards deconstructs male exploitation of the female not
only as performer but also as muse.

In 'Days', the longest story in *Rhapsody* and the last to be written,
musical ability facilitates both independence and repression for
the central female character, Leonora Morn. Here, Edwards looks
at the female psyche in more detail than in any other story in the
collection. Leonora is, on the surface at least, atypical of the female
characters in *Rhapsody* as a whole in that, as an accomplished and
professional musician, she has a successful and fulfilling career of
her own which occasions long periods of separation from her novelist
husband, George Morn. He has purchased an ugly house in a barren,
desolate location on the outskirts of the village in which he was
born, where he spends some months alone writing and preparing
the house for Leonora. Her arrival has a significant effect on his
concentration:

> During the first days after she came he worked very hard. He read
> the first few chapters to her, and this made him write more quickly.
> And she collected the loose sheets of paper on which he wrote and put
> them in order, and recopied what was necessary. He wrote neatly and
> legibly, but he inserted scraps of paper in so many places that her help
> was quite necessary. (*R*, 157)

On her arrival, Leonora immediately falls into the role of helper
or muse to her husband in a very practical sense, much as Mary
does for Sidney in 'La Penseuse', where she performs the task of
copying out Sidney's work. In 'Days', however, Edwards's manner
of presenting this situation serves to build up the impression that
it is not only Leonora's practical help that is essential to Morn's
creativity, but her very presence. His increasing activity is contrasted

starkly with her passivity: 'He could hear her practising [her music] sometimes in the drawing-room, but the rest of the time she sat with a book open on her lap, not reading, but looking at her hands or thinking' (R, 157). Morn seems to positively feed off his wife's idleness and, as he is writing, he takes comfort in her stillness.

But the arrival at the house of Leonora's composer friend, Alexander Sorel, means that her attention is increasingly drawn away from Morn and to their visitor. At one point, towards the end of the story, Sorel is writing music and Leonora attends to his practical needs, replenishing his ink supply and copying out his completed sections, much as she does for her husband. Morn, aware of this, cannot concentrate:

> Morn took the sugar-basin and went out of the room and down the stairs. He put some of the lumps of sugar into his pocket and put the basin on the bottom pillar of the balusters. He put his hand on the door-handle of the drawing-room where Leonora had begun the copying. He listened for a moment. She was whistling softly, almost under her breath. But he did not go in. He walked into his study, moved one or two papers on the table, and went and stood by the window and looked out into the darkness. The dead rose tree was just distinguishable on the lawn. He began to eat a lump of sugar. He stayed there a few minutes, and afterwards he went into the dining-room. But there was nothing there. He went out and stood at the bottom of the stairs, half meaning to go up again, but instead he took up the sugar-basin, which was still there, and carried it into the kitchen. There was no one there. (R, 186–7)

For both Morn and Sorel, Leonora acts not only as a helpmate but as muse, as a source of strength and inspiration to their creativity. Morn needs the silent attention offered by his wife in order to focus on his writing, while Leonora forms at times Sorel's inspiration. 'I thought a lot about you when I wrote the second part of the dance', he says to her of a composition he is working on (R, 193). Any sense of sexual jealousy that one would expect Morn to feel of Sorel becomes channelled instead into a creative resentment.

As the men's work flourishes, Leonora seems increasingly cut off from the world as a result of the passive state that she is forced to endure in the company of her husband and friend. 'Days' is punctuated by scenes emphasizing Leonora's calm immobility or slow movement; these scenes are usually monochrome, with greys or whites emphasized, drawing attention to the drab and dull nature of her life at home with Morn. Physical stillness seems key to Leonora's mental awareness and sense of her own life:

> It seemed to her that she had not had time to think for years. She had the curious feeling of living over again some of the days of her girlhood. There was the same quiet and solitude as then. She used in those days to have a music lesson once a week, and except for that she did nothing after her practising but sit, as now, and think. Only then she sat, as it were, at a window always looking out and always expecting something, whereas now everything was settled for her and nothing new could come from the outside. Then it was for the meaning of *her* life that she anxiously scanned the passers-by; but now, as one gets old, it is not the meaning of one's life but of life itself that one tries to understand, looking at one's hands or on the same black-and-white pages of a book. That was the difference. There seemed, too, to be something pressing heavily upon her, but it was almost pleasant not to have to throw that feeling quickly off. (*R*, 157–8; emphasis in the original)

This poignant scene is reminiscent of the ending of 'La Penseuse', where Mary sits in front of the fire 'think[ing] about her life' (*R*, 215).

Leonora embraces her isolation as a coping mechanism, leaving the men unaware of her loneliness. She appears reconciled to her isolation as an inevitable aspect of her life which, as a woman, she must endure in order to survive. A conversation with Sorel is revealing:

> 'Leonora,' he said, 'do you know I am always alone?'
> She looked down at him and did not smile. 'So am I,' she said.
> He looked again up at the sky, but without knowing it he had grasped a fold of her white dress in his hand. (*R*, 192–3)

Sorel, with his revelation of being always alone, still unconsciously but somewhat desperately makes an attempt at human contact, holding a piece of Leonora's skirt like a child clinging on to its mother. Leonora, however, makes no response.

For Sorel, Leonora offers a model of the strength and fortitude that he is himself lacking. Sorel is irrational, needy, overly emotional and susceptible to sudden rushes of feeling; in short, he is given the attributes traditionally ascribed in patriarchal discourse to women. In contrast, Leonora is able to control her emotions: she is logical and rational. In 'Days', as in *Rhapsody* as a whole, Edwards uses music to suggest the male's vision of the female in the sense that he sees what he wants to see, and not the reality. In a scene that takes place towards the end of the story, Leonora and Sorel play for Morn and his friend Mr Carmen a Greek dance that Sorel has composed:

> Sorel sat that the piano and looked round at her. The cello rested against her white dress. Her head was bent in an attitude of strength and the position of her arms gave her shoulders breadth. There is something strange about a woman playing the cello. Women like sibyls, with strength like iron, do not exist any more. Goddesses now are whisps of things. But there are still women who play the cello. She began to play the Greek dance.
>
> All the time while Sorel played . . . he could see Leonora quite clearly in the air in front of him. (*R*, 179–80)

Leonora's performance underlines Sorel's view of her as a strong, dependable woman, not as a sexual being in the way that, for example, Mr Everett in 'Rhapsody' or Mr Gallon in 'Cultivated People' view performing women. But just like Everett and Gallon, Sorel sees Leonora in the role in which he has cast her and not that which she in reality occupies: this scene is not one of female strength, as it initially appears, but of male voyeurism. As Christopher Meredith has suggested, Sorel is 'the temporary point of view'; it is his interpretation of Leonora that we see, the 'strong female archetype' that he needs, and not necessarily the reality of Leonora's character or her situation.[15]

The apparently strong, calm Leonora, then, is as silenced as Edwards's other women. She is allowed some independence when apart from her husband, but when they are together (indeed, when Leonora is in the presence of any male) she is expected to devote her full attention to him at the expense of her selfhood. Edwards's women endure an enforced passivity as a result of the patriarchal society in which they live. Although Leonora is expected to aid both her husband and her male friend in their artistic ventures, she is allowed no creative outlet herself – her role is solely to aid and interpret their male creativity – and even her musical ability is in effect an extension of this. In this story, Leonora is a mediator of creativity for the benefit of the male on several levels: she performs the mundane tasks that are above the notice of the creative males, and she channels their creativity so that it becomes available for (male) enjoyment without risk to the masculine identity (without risk of the male becoming effeminate), whilst still occupying a 'safe' female role that does not challenge the status quo.

When considered in the context of *Rhapsody* as a whole, and especially in the light of the fate of Mrs Everett in the title story and the owner's wife in 'A Country House', Leonora's situation may hold some hope. Unlike Mary in 'La Penseuse', for example, Leonora has achieved an independence unlike any other of Edwards's women, and her isolation is merely a method by which to deal with her prescribed social role so as not to be overwhelmed by male dominance. It could be argued that the period of Leonora's life represented in 'Days' is merely an interlude – she will return to her career, albeit 'off-stage'. But it is precisely the necessity of having to embrace the loneliness, the isolation, the suppression of selfhood in order to operate effectively in such a society that Edwards criticizes. Ultimately, even an ostensibly strong female character like Leonora is not impervious to the strain of adhering to the role that her society demands. By the end of 'Days' it becomes clear that Leonora, lacking the nurturing support that she is required to lavish on her husband and friend, and denied the possibility of expression through her own creativity, is like the rose tree in her husband's garden:

> He [Morn] worked in a room at the back of the house, by a window looking on to a lawn of coarse grass, in the middle of which was a dead rose tree. There was no shelter there and no bud ever came on the tree. But Morn never noticed it. (*R*, 156–7)

By mimicking a male voice in her fiction, Edwards, far from aspiring to a masculine mode of expression, emphasizes the silence of the female in patriarchal society and offers a mode of explicitly feminist writing. While Edwards's men reveal their weaknesses and idiosyncrasies by saying too much, the very voicelessness of her female characters speaks volumes.

3

Season of discontent: class barriers and their consequences in *Winter Sonata*

In a 1926 letter to Beryl Jones, Edwards indicates the extent to which musical form influenced the style and tone of the short stories included in *Rhapsody*:

> At this point I am restraining with great difficulty a desire to perform a little puzzle upon this blameless page showing the repetition of details in the different stories. I won't do the puzzle . . . but I must explain what I mean though I am afraid it is rather silly when I think of it – I mean only the mushrooms in <u>Conquered</u> and <u>Cult People</u>, Laurel holding Leonora's dress in <u>Summertime</u> [*sic*] and Sorel holding Leonora's in the nameless one ['Days'], & that sort of thing. I feel that the stories are quite inseparable from each other in the same way that the parts of a musical composition are connected, & I do want a name for the book which will express that.[1]

But it would appear that the title *Rhapsody*, suitable as it seems because of its musical associations, was arrived at in a more arbitrary fashion than one would imagine. 'I can't think of any thing particularly expressive but I have decided if they will let me to call the whole volume "Treachery in a Forest"', she says in one letter;[2] in another, she claims, 'I said to Wishart & Co "Oh dear I don't know. Call it whatever you like." And they called it *Rhapsody*.'[3] And yet it is the case that, as the quotation above indicates, Edwards's love and extensive knowledge of music greatly influenced the style and tone of her writing. Nowhere is this more evident than in her 1928 novel *Winter Sonata*, which constitutes a unique attempt to construct a work of fiction based on a musical structure.

Inspired by the success of *Rhapsody* and her experiences abroad, Edwards began writing *Winter Sonata* as soon as she had finished 'Days'. In a letter to Jones from Vienna in 1926, she summarized her novel's intended plot:

> I have begun the novel, only just begun . . . There is an old man who plays the organ in church who gives music lessons & he goes every other evening to visit a gentleman of Welsh descent who lives there – but every evening that is not an other he goes to the inn which is called the Golden Bell & goes home drunk. And his friend is suddenly ordered abroad for his health & his two nieces come to live in the house, so the organist instead of rapidly drinking himself to death, now visits them. When I have invented a respectable way of getting them there there will be two men also in the house – a fat little man – perhaps another uncle & another man, a friend of the elder sister. He is the hero. You must understand that it is winter & all the trees are black, with no leaves on them. There is the nephew of the post-master who has come to the country for his health, & is the telegraphist there. He plays the cello & is very shy & has rather a long neck. He admires the elder sister very much. The organist takes him there to play. The organist lodges with a woman who has a daughter of 16, a bit of a huzzy in an innocent sort of way & he teaches her to sing. Imagine her singing Hugo Wolf's New Years Song in Church. She embarrasses the telegraphist fearfully by giggling at him. The elder sister gives her an old frock of orange colour. The hero has such a pleasant winter – there are three girls & all different. The uncle writes to them that he is going to marry a lady that he has met there. Soon afterwards they hear that he is dead. Of course the girls must go away, & the organist will go every evening now to the <u>Golden Bell</u>. I hope it will turn out alright.[4]

While the minutiae of the novel that Edwards eventually produced are quite different from those outlined above – the gritty atmosphere of the Golden Bell inn is exchanged for yet another modernist drawing room and the ethnic implications of the uncle's Welsh descent replaced by the non-specific but apparently English backdrop – the atmosphere that Edwards aimed to achieve, with the virtually monochrome, dormant ambiance, remains unchanged. In this novel, even as it stands, Edwards finally chooses to depict working-class characters far more relevant to her own background than those drawn in *Rhapsody*.

The impermeable nature of class boundaries is key to the plot of the novel, and continual contrast is drawn between the very different worlds inhabited by its working- and middle-class characters. Divided into four chapters, or 'movements', the novel depicts the interactions between the young telegraph clerk, Arnold Nettle, and a middle-class family that lives on the outskirts of the village to which he has very recently moved. The family with which Nettle lodges – the explosive Mrs Clark, her indolent 17-year-old daughter Pauline, and young son Alexander – represent the working class. Nettle is the link between the two households – although nominally part of the Clarks' world, he aches to belong to the sphere of sophistication and leisure that for him the Nerans epitomize, and is a typical Edwards character in his isolation. Physically frail and emotionally vulnerable, he hopes that the country atmosphere will be far kinder to his health than another town winter, but he spends much of the second and third sections of the novel bed-ridden as a result of an unspecified complaint which causes him to feel tired, lethargic and depressed. This time he spends daydreaming about Olivia, the elder of the two Neran sisters and a member of the extended middle-class family that Nettle reveres, whose higher social status is reflected in the elevated position occupied by their large white house, which sits on a hill overlooking the village. Olivia and her 17-year-old sister, Eleanor, share their home with their snobbish and obnoxious aunt, Mrs Curle, and her rather pompous but inoffensive son, George. The family is joined for the second and third movements of the novel by George's literary critic friend, David Premiss. '[R]ather accustomed to feminine admiration' and considering himself to be 'devoted to the most important things in life . . . the "higher things"', Premiss is as interesting a character from the point of view of gender as of class (WS 106, 108). Charming but fickle, he remains true to Edwards's initial vision of her ironic 'hero', spending his time flirting, in very different ways, with the 'three girls & all different', Eleanor, Olivia and Pauline.

Nettle's position as a working man is emphasized from the outset of Winter Sonata, when he is shown leaving his lodgings for the post office where he is employed. In this opening scene, Pauline

Clark and her young brother, Alexander, demonstrate the un-inhibited behaviour later to be revealed as characteristic of their family. Deceived by the unseasonable warmth of a mild day in early winter, Alexander 'took off his dress in the middle of the road'; Pauline 'slapped him until he cried' (*WS*, 2), then left him sobbing on the pavement while she contrived to steal a glance at their new lodger:

> She went in and asked for a telegraph form. Arnold Nettle gave it to her. He was a strange young man, and much better dressed than any of the choirboys. She smiled at him, and then looked down at her feet and began scraping one of them on the floor. She looked up again as if she could not help laughing at him. He blushed. (*WS*, 2–3)

Into this scene of everyday working-class life comes Olivia Neran, clothed in a pure white woollen dress. She drifts in and out again silently, unobtrusively, in contrast to Pauline who stares conspicu-ously after her 'interested . . . only in her dress. Both the Neran sisters always had nice dresses, and they were moreover pretty' (*WS*, 3). Nettle finds himself drawn to Olivia, a highly significant development for him, as his usual emotional state is one of loneliness and disconnection; he does not feel at home anywhere, not even when he is with his uncle and his family:

> [At his uncle's home] he sat quietly and only answered their inquiries and smiled at them without feeling in any way at home there . . . But if he ever met any of the people from Olivia's house, then he was very happy to be with them and heard everything they said as though it were important and of significance for his own life, as if they were in a way beings from another world . . . they really were people whose life was in every way different from his, while Pauline and her mother and Alexander were quite ordinary things in his life, and were painted in the dull colours of everything that is too near. (*WS*, 37–8)

Nettle is first invited to visit the Nerans' home by Mrs Curle, who, if she 'ever saw anybody in the village who, she believed, could entertain her in any way . . . hurriedly made his acquaintance'

(*WS*, 7). When Mrs Curle is made aware that Nettle can play the cello, she invites him up to the house to perform for the family:

> Mrs Curle walked along slowly, looking in front of her, and she went past Mr Nettle, but then, evidently because the form of the cello had impressed itself on her mind, she stopped and looked back. She took hold of her son's arm to bring him back with her and returned a few paces . . .
> 'Do you play that?' she asked.
> Holding the cello in a tight embrace, Mr Nettle smiled, and said, 'Yes.'
> 'We are going for a walk,' began George Curle conversationally, but his mother interrupted him and said urgently, 'You must come up some evening to play to us. What time does the post-office shut?'
> 'Six o'clock,' said Mr Nettle.
> 'I will send and let you know on which day,' she said, beginning to walk on . . .
> Mr Nettle looked after them in some astonishment. (*WS*, 8)

This is a characteristically comic scene, and Mrs Curle is one of Edwards's most harshly drawn characters. Physically she is 'rather fat, and also she looked a bit like a goose, and just as a goose looks cruel in a stupid way she had that expression too' (*WS*, 6). With no redeeming feature, she is rude, ignorant and only interested in others for their entertainment value; during Nettle's first visit to the house she demands of him, 'Is there anyone else in the village who can play or do anything?' (*WS*, 13). Through her interactions with Nettle, and later Pauline, it becomes apparent that Mrs Curle feels that such civilities as courtesy and respect need not be extended to those below her on the social scale. But, for Nettle, the Nerans and the Curles epitomize breeding, beauty and social distinction, and he is blind to the arrogance and social snobbery that they also demonstrate.

In fact, Nettle himself maintains and reinforces such class boundaries in his response to the Clark family, and especially Pauline, whom he considers to be beneath his notice, for '[a]lthough Mr Nettle lived with these people . . . he could not be said to be interested in them at all' (*WS*, 37). Nettle visits the Neran home several times, and is beginning to feel himself their friend when, in their quest for entertainment, the family, and Premiss in particular, insist that Nettle invite Pauline to the house to sing. The invasion of the every-day into his dreamland threatens to shatter his illusion, and '[h]e felt suddenly angry at Pauline's intrusion into this quite different world' (*WS*, 47). Extremely reluctant to convey the invitation to Pauline, he does so in a rather commanding manner:

> She came into his room to clear away the tea-things, and he said, 'Miss Neran would like you to go up there and sing a song for them.'
> 'Which Miss Neran?' she asked.
> 'All of them up at the house,' he said, a little impatiently.
> She half smiled. 'When?' she asked.
> 'You are to go up there Thursday evening, about seven o'clock. Take something with you to sing. You are not to stay there long, you know,' he added in explanation, 'but just sing a song or two, and then go home.'
> Pauline considered this in silence. She was perfectly satisfied with the idea, and did not take his advice at all in bad part. (*WS*, 88–9)

During their visit, Nettle tries his best to disassociate himself from Pauline, to the extent that he 'deliberately waited for half an hour after she had gone [up to the Nerans' house] before he started' (*WS*, 89). The discomfort he experiences as a result of Pauline's presence is perhaps a consequence of his suppressed but uncomfort-able awareness of his own class position. When Pauline is also present in the Neran household, he cannot so easily fool himself into thinking that he shares their world: 'he felt rather angry, though by this time he was not sure why. He did not somehow feel as happy there as he used to' (*WS*, 91).

In the company of the Neran and Curle families Pauline's lower-class status becomes even more apparent. Her songbook is 'torn and dirty' and when Premiss asks her if she can sing any Bach, she looks at him 'blankly, because she did not know the names of the composers' (*WS*, 90). It is, of course, hardly surprising that Pauline does not share the awareness of the Neran circle of the social propri-eties upheld in middle-class society. The fact that Eleanor and Pauline are the same age serves to emphasize how social difference has directed their experiences. At seventeen years old, Eleanor has just left school and spends her time reading, walking and sitting idly in the drawing room, while Pauline appears to have had little formal education and is destined for a life of servitude and domestic drudgery. Yet, despite her apparent vulgarity and ignorance, Pauline shows a far more incisive appreciation of art than the Nerans would credit her with, as when performing in the church choir:

> It seemed to her that the organist was an old fool, but she liked to hear him play the organ. She would stop singing to hear him, and she knew she could never sing like that, like a great strong pillar reaching up to heaven. (WS, 17)

Like the women in *Rhapsody*, Nettle and Pauline are merely purveyors of music for the enjoyment of the Neran household, and are considered to be ignorant of the aesthetic value of their own music because of their social standing. In a conversation with Olivia, Eleanor says of Nettle: 'you know, considering that he probably knows nothing at all about it, it seems to me he plays really rather decently' (WS, 29). Little has changed in her attitude by the end of the novel: when handing Nettle a book of essays written by Premiss, '"You must tell us what you think of it," she said kindly, though she did not really think that he would be able to give an opinion on it' (WS, 238–9). As the sole members of the ruling class in their village, the family consider themselves to be the only people qualified to appreciate art and culture, yet they do not actually participate themselves (except for Olivia, who accompanies Nettle and Pauline on the piano); they are merely voyeurs, just like Mr Everett in 'Rhapsody', suggesting a specific parallel between class-based and gender-based subjugation. As Susan McClary suggests, '[s]truggles over musical propriety are themselves political struggles over whose music, whose images of pleasure or beauty, whose rules of order shall prevail'.[5]

Unlike Nettle, Pauline Clark is fully aware of her status in the village and the nuances of her role as performer for the Nerans' pleasure. She does not expect any form of friendship, and is prepared to leave once she has completed her allotted task: '[s]he sang two more songs. She knew then that it was time for her to go' (*WS*, 92). Nettle, however, is unable to appreciate the nature of his association with the Neran household, attributing his connection with them to his imagined bond with Olivia rather than the dull nature of their idle lives and their constant desire for entertainment. He thinks, '[i]t must have been because she [Olivia] spoke of him at home that he was first asked up there – to play, too, of course, but that was as good a way as another of beginning an acquaintance' (*WS*, 51). To most of the Neran household at least, Nettle is little more than a diversion to be called on in times of boredom. On the sole occasion that he calls at the house uninvited, and without his cello, the family is surprised at the intrusion despite the fact that George, Mrs Curle and even Eleanor all call on Nettle uninvited at times. Their treatment of Pauline Clark is very similar if a little more transparent. Pauline goes for a walk past the house one afternoon only to be found by Mrs Curle, who to all intents and purposes orders Pauline to go in and sing for the rest of the family. Eleanor's response is: 'That's fine. We were wondering how to amuse ourselves' (*WS*, 111).

As much as he tries to align himself with George, Olivia and the rest, it is their very difference that forms the basis of their appeal for Nettle. Rather than try to cross or even destroy class boundaries, an action that could ultimately result in a closer connection with Olivia, he instead reinforces their superior social status by admiring them from afar. When speaking to George, 'it impressed him very much to realise how these people who seemed to him not to possess any of the customary human failings should be so full of humility' (*WS*, 228). And when George (who considers himself to be a student of philosophy, although he is as idle as his cousins) is 'despondent . . . about his work . . . Nettle would have liked to reassure him in some manner but he could find no way of expressing his feelings about George's immense learning and cleverness' (*WS*, 226). Nettle clings to the established social order; even his dreams have connotations of social distinctions. The sensation of a particularly vivid dream remains with him for some time, and during the following day he recalls:

There had been a large shield, with arms of some kind on it . . . The shield was very big, as high as a man . . . But the important thing was, of course, the extraordinary emotional significance this shield had for him . . . he could see quite clearly a hand mailed in silver holding the great shield . . . against the rush of thousands of bright silver spears . . . the ground . . . was disturbed everywhere with the prints of horses' hoofs, [and he stood looking] at a garland of white flowers made to fit a woman's head. (WS, 67, 69, 71)

The suggestion is that Nettle appears in his dream as an adoring knight protecting the old world of feudal rank, a system even more rigid than the social divisions presented in the text, against the onslaught of the modern world, for the sake of his mistress or queen Olivia, represented in his dream by the garland of white flowers that rests on the ground – Nettle had previously revealed that he 'always saw her [Olivia] with a garland of white flowers around her head' (WS, 49).

In the final scene of the novel, Nettle has recovered from his winter illness enough to resume his visits to the Neran household, where his admiration apparently reaches new heights:

They sat around the table like stars, and when they spoke their voices seemed to come to him from far away, as though by some chance the heavens had opened for a minute and a fragment of some angelic conversation had floated down to him upon the earth. With innocent and lonely awe he listened to every word that came from their lips. (WS, 241)

Nettle's reluctance, or downright refusal, to attempt to breach the class barriers so rigidly enforced in his society is in part the source of his depression and illness and contributes to his marginalized position: his failure to act translates into his physically disabled condition. During his illness, Nettle and Mrs Curle have a rather absurd encounter that, when repeated at the end of the novel, serves to highlight the very real nature of the boundary between Nettle and the occupants of the white house:

One day when Mrs Curle was passing his house she saw him in the window. He was standing there looking out. She went up and spoke to him, but since the window was closed he could not hear what she was saying and looked rather alarmed and worried, and since it did not at first occur to him to go and open the door they stood there, rather stupidly, without being able to communicate. (*WS*, 179)

Nettle and Mrs Curle are unable to communicate as a result of the literal barrier between them (the glass); neither of them is able to identify the simple way of resolving this (opening the window). This image is repeated in the final scene of the novel, when Nettle leaves the Nerans' house:

'Do you prefer to leave by the window or the door?' she [Eleanor] asked smiling, as George came up to them.

Nettle, taking the suggestion seriously, obediently climbed over the window-sill, and stood on the grass waiting to say goodbye. (*WS*, 244)

Although Nettle has literally crossed the (invisible) boundary that had previously prevented his communication with Mrs Curle, he has done so on the basis of his inability to interpret Eleanor's bantering tone – he does so 'obediently' – rather than making any real attempt to set his relationship with the family on a level footing. At the end of the novel, he remains as much in awe of them as ever.

Nettle's fascination with Olivia, then, operates on the basis of her perceived superiority to him, rather than his physical or emotional response to her. There is no hint of lust in this sickly young man. His 'nameless fear of girls' means that he is terrified by any expression of female sexuality (*WS*, 3), and as a result he finds Pauline and her blatant sexual curiosity embarrassing and confusing. Pauline is by far the most overtly sexual of Edwards's women, and represents a departure from the staid and invalid females of *Rhapsody*.[6] Her curiosity about Nettle soon wanes when she discovers that he is impervious to her feminine wiles, but she finds another way of making use of him as an unwilling aid to her late-night escapades with the local lads:

Pauline had found, after all, that Mr Nettle was not very interesting, and for this reason she made him useful. It was more fun to go round with the choir-boys ... More than once, when he [Nettle] was getting ready to go up [to bed], he heard Pauline's light tap on the window. He pulled up the blind and she signed to him to let her in. (*WS*, 16, 24)

Pauline's life, punctuated only by conflict with her mother and her fleeting late-night encounters with the choirboys (and later her early-morning walks with Premiss), is a cycle of hard manual labour:

Her mother came to wake her so early that it was still dark. Often she had to be dragged out of bed; she hated being awakened ... She went downstairs and did the work she had to do, but she sulked all the morning. She sulked until there was a chance to go out to the shop and see people. She would stay out as long as she dared, and when she got home her mother would give it to her, call her 'a huzzy; a good-for-nothing; a slut.' (*WS*, 18)

Pauline's relationship with her mother is volatile and explosive, and very different from the strained and tense but always stiflingly proper middle-class relationships that characterize Edwards's fiction. Mrs Clark thinks little of chastising Pauline, both physically and verbally, in public, much to the disturbance of both Nettle and Eleanor Neran (*WS*, 214). This is the only mother-daughter relationship in Edwards's *oeuvre*; it is as startling as it is telling in its complexity and may well owe something to Edwards's relationship with her own mother. Like Pauline, Edwards felt that she was constantly harangued over domestic tasks: 'From morning to night I am likely at any moment to be rowed – though not very ferociously – for anything', she said in a letter to college friend Sona Rosa Burstein.[7]

But Edwards's treatment of Pauline is sympathetic as well as rigorous. Pauline appears uncouth, undisciplined, nosy, insolent and lazy, but she is judged entirely by the social standards of others and, at times, there is an overriding suggestion that she is merely a misunderstood young woman. Her insolent half smile, for example, could be as a result of shyness: 'Pauline smiled up at him [George] in her rather insolent way. It may have been from gratitude' (*WS*,

179). Pauline's attention seeking may be an attempt to replace the lack of affection shown to her by her mother and her interest in the Neran sisters is an escape from her unremittingly bleak daily routine. Her interest in the choirboys and Mr Premiss may constitute a search for a male role-model or paternal figure: Pauline's father does not appear in *Winter Sonata*, and there is a suggestion that his absence is a source of much pain and discomfort to the family. When Mrs Clark sees her daughter return from an early morning walk with Premiss, her reaction suggests that her husband's absence is the result of some sexual misconduct:

> [Mrs Clark to Pauline]: 'You mark my words; you'll get into trouble some day . . . You're like your father, that's what you are. No daughter of mine ought to behave like that.'
> 'What did my father do?' asked Pauline, looking her straight in the eyes, and smiling impudently, because she knew very well.
> Her mother bit her lip and got red.
> 'Never you mind what your father did,' she said. 'He's dead now.'
> Pauline smiled her disbelief, and her mother, becoming suddenly more angry than she had been before, slapped her face with all her force. (*WS*, 129)

Mrs Clark's violent reaction to her daughter's behaviour may after all be motivated by love and the need to protect: Pauline, in her innocence and curiosity, places herself in precarious situations, the danger of which her mother is all too aware of as a result of her own experiences.

The gifts that Eleanor and Olivia give to Pauline during her visits emphasize her subordinate status and their privilege, and also signal her entry into a market of exchange. An initial gift of a box of chocolates is soon followed by a few drops of perfume, an orange dress from Olivia and a long string of green beads which Eleanor contrives to present to Pauline, naively, in the street (*WS*, 156). 'Thank you, *and* for the scent', Pauline says to Olivia, gratefully enough (*WS*, 115; emphasis in the original). In *Sisters and Rivals in British Women's Fiction, 1914–1939* (2000), Diana Wallace discusses the construction of class within gendered paradigms in Rebecca West's *The Return of the Soldier* (1918). In this novel an upper-class soldier, Chris Baldry, returns from fighting on the front line. Having lost all memory of the last fifteen years, he demands to be reunited with his first love, Margaret Allington, now married and living in a cramped terraced house on the outskirts of the nearby industrial town. Baldry's cold wife, Kitty, a perfect example of the Victorian 'angel in the house', and his cousin Jenny, the narrator, contrive to maintain a distance from Margaret which is grounded in class difference, regardless of their shared gender. Wallace argues: '[t]o admit their similarity, their shared oppressed status, with the suffragette or the working-class woman, would be to relinquish the power and protection they gain from their class status as "ladies"'.[8] This argument applies equally well to Olivia and Eleanor's treatment of Pauline Clark. The sisters reinforce Pauline's inferior class status through their kindly but patronizing bestowal of gifts which emphasize the fact that although they are of the same sex, Pauline, as a result of her social grouping, is very different.

The pleasure that Pauline and her brother Alexander derive from these somewhat luxurious gifts demonstrates Edwards's skill at depicting the nuances and innocence of the young siblings (a technique rehearsed in 'A Throne in Heaven'), and highlights the barren, pleasureless nature of their lives. Alexander is overawed by the mysterious gifts that his sister brings home, despite their overtly feminine nature: when Pauline gives him the perfume-drenched handkerchief, he 'smelt it, looking up at her over it, and when she began to take it away he put his hand up to keep it there for still another moment' (*WS*, 117). The orange dress, too, occasions a similar reaction in Alexander; when he sees Pauline in the gown 'his wonder made his eyes wider and wider', and he continually peeps into a trunk where Pauline hides the garment for fear of reprisal from her mother (*WS*, 116–17, 118). The following day, Pauline takes the dress to Nettle's room in order to try it on in front of his mirror, where it rests on his bed 'like something strange and not altogether belonging to the place' (*WS*, 118), its bright colour suggesting a vitality that the characters of the novel – with the exception, perhaps, of Pauline herself – lack.

Edwards's selection of prefatory poem for the volume is particularly suggestive in the light of her depiction of class-based social conventions in the novel. The composer of 'Lob des Winters', Middle High German poet Walter von der Vogelweide (*c*.1170–*c*.1230), was an innovative lyricist who wrote on the subject of courtly love and consummated relationships. The poem, which Edwards quotes in the original middle German, translates as:[9]

> Winter has a short day,
> But a long night
> So that the lover from love may
> Rest while day is awake.
> What have I said?
> Oh dear, had I been quiet,
> I should always lie like this.
>
> (Hât der Winter kurzen tac
>   sô hat er die langen naht
> daz sich liep bî liebe mac
>   wol erholn, daz ê dâ vaht.
> Wâz hân ich gesprochen? owê jâ
>   haete ich baz geswigen
>   sol ich iemer sô geligen.)[10]

This poem, initially at least, appears to have little relevance to the stiflingly dull lives which form the subject matter of *Winter Sonata*, and serves to reinforce the restrictive and ultimately unhealthy nature of divisive class structures in the novel. In fact, the only character who engages in any sort of genuine physical human contact such as that being experienced by the first-person speaker of the poem is Pauline Clark. Her antics with the choirboys are suggestive of sexual curiosity and its potential exploration:

> On choir-practice nights, as soon as the clock struck seven, even if she were in the middle of some work, she would put everything down and run across to the church . . . After the practice she ran out of the churchyard like a little cat and walked slowly up the road pretending she liked to take a walk by herself . . . in winter it was already dark, and almost before she turned the corner she

could walk slowly, and some of the boys would follow her . . . (*WS*, 16–17)

The following morning, Pauline must be 'dragged out of bed' by her mother, deprived of the morning's slumber so important to Vogelweide's narrator, who rests 'while day is awake' (*WS*, 18). The only compensation that Pauline receives for her early rising is the opportunity to meet with Premiss, whom she finds even more fascinating than her choirboys:

> [Pauline] saw Mr Premiss pass the house as if he were going for a walk, for it was a fine though cold morning. She ran down a road which would lead her back to the main road, along which he was walking, without her having to pass him . . . He was just turning the corner and coming towards her. Her heart gave two big thumps. (*WS*, 83)

Premiss has an intricate knowledge of the class systems in society, their boundaries and how to manipulate them. Pauline naively but blatantly seeks any sort of male attention; Premiss, on his part, is happy to flirt with and even kiss her. By directing his attentions at Pauline rather than Eleanor or Olivia (he attempts only a light flirtation with the two sisters, to which Olivia seems impervious) he escapes the threat of marriage, or indeed of any serious emotional engagement, that would inevitably present itself had he approached either of the Neran sisters in the same manner. But Premiss, who sees himself as something of a daring flirt, is curiously void of passion during his encounters with Pauline. Like Nettle, he appears strangely desexualized, and his physical appearance (he is 'rather short and exceedingly pale' (*WS*, 72)) is suggestive of a lack of vigour and strength. His attentions towards Pauline are apparently driven by a detached anthropological interest, rather than any sexual urge:

> He began to push the hair back inside her collar, and, since she showed no reluctance, laughing with immense amusement, he kissed her once or twice. He stood looking at her to see what effect it had produced, but she was looking at him equally attentively to see if he was going to kiss her again. (*WS*, 100)

Premiss treats each of the three girls, Oliva, Eleanor and Pauline, precisely in the manner that their social position dictates: with Olivia, the elder of the two Neran sisters, he is largely respectful yet lightly flirtatious; with Eleanor, the younger sister, he is far more suggestive but operates within the boundaries; but Pauline is considered free game as a result of her working-class position. Premiss likens Pauline's temperament to that of a bacchante, emphasizing his view of her as an overly sexualized and physical, not intellectual, being (*WS*, 121), just as the owner in 'A Country House' viewed his wife as a potentially deviant creature (*R*, 35). When she sings for the family '[i]t gave him immense pleasure to hear the voice of Bach's Virgin come from Pauline's lips', relishing the irony of the scene given Pauline's sexual interest in him (*WS*, 112).

It is appropriate that Pauline, rather than the Neran sisters, becomes the owner of the orange dress; throughout the text she is represented as a source of colour, energy and warmth, in contrast to the winter chill of their environment. She and her family do not suffer the continual self-repression endured by the occupants of the Neran household. Pauline consistently acts on her instincts, as does her brother. In the opening scene of the novel in which he removes his clothing as a result of the unseasonable heat, he is responding directly to his physical surroundings without fear of impropriety or reprisal (*WS*, 2). A physical and emotional existence, it appears, is ultimately far less stultifying than a cultured but repressive middle-class way of life.

By virtue of their class, then, Eleanor and Olivia appear to be prevented from expressing spontaneous human feeling and emotion in the way that Pauline does. Eleanor (whose name is a version of Leonora, linking her to her namesakes in 'Summer-time' and 'Days') quotes Dante Gabriel Rossetti's 'Known in Vain' to George:[11] 'but sitting oft / Together within hopeless sight of hope / For hours are silent' (*WS*, 171). 'You can't say that isn't beautiful', she says (*WS*, 171). As poignant as Eleanor's chosen lines may be, they are also evocative of the situation in which she and her sister find themselves as a result of their status as middle-class ladies. Olivia and Nettle are 'Together within hopeless sight of hope' as a result of their refusal to cross the class boundaries that preclude them from the possibility of a relationship with each other. The subsequent lines from Rossetti's poem: 'When Work and Will awake too late, to gaze / After their life sailed by, and hold their breath' ring true for Olivia, if not for her sister, as she finds herself trapped in a perpetual hibernation.[12]

In *Winter Sonata*, far more attention is lavished on descriptions of the scenery than in any of Edwards's other works. The backdrop against which the characters move is often presented in some detail, generally in a wintry monochrome, as in the following passage:

> The sky was uniformly *grey*, not *dark* with rain-clouds, but *grey* with no *white* in it anywhere. On either side of the *white* road the bare hedges and sometimes the *grey*, naked branches of a leafless tree over-shadowed it a little. Some *grey* sheep moved about silently in the fields. Down in the hollow below the road, where a stream ran, the trees looked *black* and like little feathery clouds, and far upon the other side bracken lay in broad *brown* patches on the *pale*, short grass. (*WS*, 21; my emphasis)

Such use of a monochrome backdrop emphasizes the lethargic tone of the novel. The landscape is void of colour and serves as a base; often in such scenes colour is introduced, slowly and deliberately – the green of the fir trees, the reddish streaks of a rising or setting sun. The repeated image of the black trees and their golden leaves epitomize the coming winter; the scene is beautiful, but bare and barren, with none of the vitality of the summer months. This detailed impressionistic technique is one that Edwards returns to again and again, so much so that she says of herself in a letter to Beryl Jones 'I begin to suspect the ease with which I handle scenery.'[13] In her 1929 review of *The Landscape of Thomas Hardy* by Donald Maxwell, Edwards indicates the importance to her of such a technique in literature. 'The landscape in Thomas Hardy's novels is more than a background for the story. It is much more than this – it is even more important to the plot than any of the characters; it is rather the chief character', she notes.[14] This is precisely how landscape is treated in *Winter Sonata*.

Olivia consistently reflects, both in appearance and character, the wintry palette that comes to dominate the novel. From the outset she has been associated with the bleak and barren winter landscape: she first appears in a white woollen dress, and '[a]s she came down between the bare grey trees and along the hard grey road it was difficult to tell whether the white figure was more like summer going sadly away from the earth or like winter stealing quietly upon it' (WS, 3). Her 'round pale face' with its 'large dark eyes' (WS, 28) reflects the monochrome landscape that surrounds her home. She becomes associated with the fir trees that stand on sentry outside her front door and populate the surrounding landscape: Premiss, for example, says to her 'I will think of you every time I see a fir tree' (WS, 138). But this association with the fir is not necessarily positive: despite their potential to represent a sense of continuous life as a result of their evergreen nature (they contrast starkly with the bare barren skeletons of the deciduous trees that surround them), in their association with Olivia they come to represent the unchanging, static nature of her existence: they do not participate in the seasonal change so essential to life. The novel's German epigraph suggests that seasonal change and the potential for prolonged close contact that winter provides is essential to ensure new life in spring. But as a hint of spring approaches, Olivia becomes increasingly withdrawn and reflective:

> Olivia went in these days for walks by herself, thinking and even dreaming as she went along between the delicate black lacework of the leafless hedges under the soft grey sky, or she sat in the house with her hands lying idle on her lap, not reading or doing anything. She felt . . . a certain lassitude of mind which made her scarcely desire to talk to anyone or even to read, and she sat most of the day without moving, her hands lying idle in her lap. (WS, 133, 183)

Olivia's mental passivity begins to manifest itself in a physical stillness, in a similar manner to that experienced by Leonora Morn in 'Days'. Like Leonora, Olivia spends much of her time sitting with her hands in her lap, an image that emphasizes her passive nature (her hands are literally still) as well as the suggestion that there is nothing more to her life, and shows the destructive effects of enforced passivity on the female psyche. In contrast to Olivia, the male characters are restless and searching: George Curle is continually in pursuit of the meaning of his life, and often takes out the frustration caused by his existential angst on his mother, who cites ambition as the source of her late husband's discontent: 'he was very ambitious, and that never made him do anything out of the ordinary; it simply made him impatient', she tells George of his father (WS, 161). Olivia, on the other hand, is aware of the value of contemplation over ambition. She says to George: 'I think perhaps if one could learn to be absolutely receptive of every sensation and every impression as it comes, without any reference to what one expects, or to what one wants, one would be perfectly happy' (WS, 168).

But in Olivia's case, with no outlet of expression, her passivity results in fatigue and eventually depression. Indeed, she seems to be experiencing a form of emotional hibernation as a result of the continual repression of her physical and emotional needs. As a 'proper lady', she is required by society to behave in a predefined manner: to be passive, observant of social proprieties, elegant and well-dressed. She adheres to this role perfectly but, it appears, at the cost of her selfhood. Olivia's repression is underlined throughout the novel, not only by means of her association with the winter landscape, but through Edwards's sustained and suggestive use of the Greek myth of Persephone's abduction.[15] The scenery in which the Neran household stands is presented from Premiss's point of view:

> the leafless trees were indeed extraordinarily beautiful just here in all their misty colours of black, grey, brown, and sometimes a curious red. Here and there among them was the dark, deep green of fir trees which seemed to stand down there among the shades like heroes who alone can descend living into Hades. Somewhere in their midst, half concealed by their bare lifeless branches, was the wonderfully delicate green of a young fir, like a strange little maiden who had wandered by some mischance into that baneful place, like poor Persephone herself, with her beauty obscured and veiled by joyless shadows. (WS, 193–4)

In the Homeric *Hymn to Demeter*, Persephone's father, Zeus, has agreed with his brother Pluto, king of the underworld, Hades, that Persephone will be his wife.[16] Zeus sends a beautiful narcissus to trap Persephone: while out with her maiden kin, she plucks the flower and Pluto rises up from the underworld to claim his queen and take her back down into Hades. Persephone's mother Demeter, goddess of corn, not consulted in the fraternal bargain, leaves the kingdom of the gods and searches the earth for her daughter but to no avail. In her grief she shows 'a terrifying capacity for destruction. She holds the seed within the earth so that no crops can grow and men starve and have no sacrifices to offer the gods.'[17] Zeus intervenes, and orders Pluto to return Persephone to her mother so that normality can be restored and sacrifices to the gods can once again be made but, while Pluto complies, he tricks Persephone into eating a pomegranate seed on her departure. As a result of Pluto's trickery, Persephone is under a spell that forces her to return to Hades every year: at this time winter falls on earth, while her return to her mother and the kingdom of the gods signals the arrival of spring. By the end of the novel Olivia is 'motionless', even her beauty is 'subdued' just as Persephone's beauty is 'obscured [and] veiled by joyless shadows' (*WS*, 194).

Edwards continues Olivia's underworld associations through her evocation of Welsh myth. Olivia is out walking one day, lost in her own thoughts, unaware that Premiss is frantically trying to catch her up. When she finally hears his calls and waits for him, he says:

> I have been trying to catch you up for miles . . . but every time I got nearer you walked more quickly than ever, and I was left behind again . . . It was like a magic spell. I felt as though some wicked fairy was keeping the distance between us always the same. No effort of mine seemed to be any good. (*WS*, 134–5)

In the first branch of the medieval Welsh myths that make up the *Mabinogi*, Pwyll, prince of Dyfed, is sitting on Gorsedd Arberth, a hill in his kingdom, when he sees 'a lady on a big fine pale white horse, with a garment of shining gold brocaded silk upon her, coming along the high-way that led past the mound'.[18] Despite the white horse's 'slow even pace',[19] several attempts to catch up with the lady fail; at last Pwyll speaks to her:

> [Pwyll] turned after her and let his horse, mettled and prancing, take its own speed. And he thought that at the second bound or the third he would come up with her. But he was no nearer to her than before. He drove his horse to its utmost speed, but he saw that it was idle for him to follow her.
>
> Then Pwyll spoke. 'Maiden,' he said, 'for his sake whom thou lovest best, stay for me.' 'I will, gladly,' said she, 'and it had been better for the horse hadst thou asked this long since.'[20]

The lady is Rhiannon of Annwn (or Annwfn), the Celtic Otherworld or Hades. Like Persephone, Rhiannon protests against a marriage arranged against her will, from which she is rescued – in Rhiannon's case, by Pwyll. But Olivia, it seems, is without rescuer: neither Premiss nor Nettle is strong enough to make a direct appeal to her and so liberate her from her underworld.

The same winter landscape, however, has a very different effect on Eleanor: it makes her feel 'like a bird whom no obstacle prevents from spreading its wings and flying to and fro over the earth' (*WS*, 205). She discovers some snowdrops in their otherwise barren and lifeless garden: '[t]here, where the thick dark branches of the little fir tree sheltered the garden from the wind, the whitish-green leaves of snowdrops were pushing their blunt tops up through the hard earth' (*WS*, 206). Olivia, with her association with the fir tree, endures her perpetual emotional and physical hibernation in part in order to protect Eleanor (represented by the snowdrops) and allow her to achieve her 'spring'. For, as Olivia's lethargy and depression grows, Eleanor 'felt very happy and gay. It seemed to her at that moment that the whole world might have been contained within herself. It made her feel as if everything around her were on the point of springing into life' (*WS*, 218). While Eleanor and George admire the snowdrops enthusiastically, Olivia is dismissive, 'looking down wearily at the little leaves' (*WS*, 206), and is assailed by a wave of the depression that increasingly affects her throughout the novel:

A sudden feeling of loneliness had come upon her, so intense, that the place and the people around her, the hard, stony garden and the trees, stood out empty and bare as though without any deeper implications, as though she had withdrawn into herself all the imagination and affection which could have given them life and depth. She felt in that moment an almost intolerable distaste for life, a kind of nausea. (*WS*, 207)

Although the earth remains cold and frozen, Eleanor's snowdrops prosper as harbingers of more growth to come:

By this time there were little green buds on Eleanor's snowdrops, and one or two yellow and purple and white crocuses were coming up right in the middle of the grass in the garden.

Eleanor, because she had nothing to do, walked along the roads and through the fields . . . she stopped and looked at the grey trees or at the tangle of bare, grey twigs in a hedge, and although there was no sign in them yet of Spring, the fact that they were really preparing to burst into life, that all that life was imprisoned in them, made them seem already not so barren and dead. For this reason she picked one without thinking and carried it home, only then realising that it was of no use, she left it lying on the garden path. (*WS*, 215–16)

Eleanor's association with the spring offers a sense of the potential for positive change and, accordingly, she questions the nature of power in society in a manner that Olivia, who represents cold, unchanging winter, cannot. For while Eleanor adheres to the social boundaries in her relations with Nettle and Pauline, she does take steps towards realizing a female solidarity, regardless of class status. In her penultimate encounter with Premiss, she engages him in a final private conversation in which, when discussing his bachelor status, he reveals his expectations of a wife's role, telling her:

'I am a very disorderly man. I have left something in every corner of the house and it takes me a terrible time to pack. It is because I am a bachelor, you know. If I had a wife it would be all right.'

'But you wouldn't let your wife do your packing for you?' said Eleanor, a little shocked by this.

'Yes, I would,' he said, looking at her solemnly.

'But you couldn't let your wife be a slave to you, Mr Premiss!'

'Yes, I could,' he said, highly amused.

She walked on in silence.

'Why, Miss Eleanor' he said, 'you are cross with me?'

'Well,' she said, gravely raising her eyes to his, 'if men as clever as you are willing to be among the oppressors of women, what can one expect of ordinary men?' (*WS*, 196–7)

Not only is Eleanor aware of the subjugated status of women in her society, but she is beginning to realize that educated middle-class men like Premiss exploit their social dominance for their own gain.

On one occasion Olivia too feels a sense of spring, but in her case the feeling of impending hope brings with it an aura of impermanence and fragility:

She felt happy. It seemed as if a new life were beginning, as though the blue sky were the beginning of spring and not only a pause in the cold greyness of the winter. She began to walk always more quickly, scarcely thinking, but hurrying on with a sensation of happiness, inexplicable and filled with that certainty of its lasting for ever, which comes just before it begins to die again. (*WS*, 134)

The last ominous clause suggests that Olivia has allowed herself to become trapped within the demands of her society whereas Eleanor, although inconsistent, has begun to demonstrate a potential for social change evident in her questioning of Premiss's view of women. Like the branch that Eleanor picks up and then discards, Olivia, and all that she has come to internalize, is eventually going to be left 'of no use'. It is as if Edwards has split the Persephone role between the two Neran sisters, with the older girl perpetually caught in a mournful winter while the younger looks forward to spring.

Edwards's use of this myth not only serves to reinforce the winter theme of the novel but also highlights the gendered nature of the society that she so critically delineates. In the original Greek context, Persephone's abduction is as a result of an arrangement between her father and her uncle; her mother is not consulted, nor is she informed. The myth can be read as an allegory of patriarchal exchange, where women are objects of value to be passed from one man to another. But it is also a story about maternal love and the connection between mother and daughter, as '[i]t is displacement and separation from her mother that Persephone complains of when she is carried off by Hades on his chariot to his realm in the lower world'.[21] For Demeter, her bond with her daughter overrides all else; it leads her to leave the kingdom of the gods and reject Zeus' offers of great powers designed to tempt her to return. As such, it also offers a framework within which to read the mother-daughter relationship between Mrs Clark and Pauline. On her daughter's return, Demeter asks whether she has eaten anything whilst in the underworld, and Persephone has to admit that Pluto forced her to eat an enchanted pomegranate seed. It is this seed within her which draws her back to the underworld. Equally, Mrs Clark's anxiety about Pauline's 'flighty' nature would appear to rise from her fear that Pauline might commit a sexual act that would result in pregnancy and tie her to one man against her will for the rest of her life. The force of her feeling can be seen in a typically violent outburst on Pauline's return from an early morning walk with Premiss:

> 'What have you been doing out all that time with him?' her mother said, looking at her with suspicious and anxious fury . . . 'Aren't you ashamed of yourself?' . . .
> 'What have I done?' shouted Pauline, beginning to sob. (*WS*, 128–9)

Mrs Clark's reaction to Pauline's evident interest in the opposite sex reflects Demeter's first question to Persephone on her return; she is afraid that Pauline too may have partaken of the dangerous seed. The conflict between them, then, can be seen as a result of the continual risk presented by selfish and irresponsible pleasure-seeking males, like Pluto and Premiss.

Stylistically, *Winter Sonata* represents a departure from *Rhapsody*: in the novel, Edwards moves away from several of the methods established in her short stories. *Winter Sonata* is narrated entirely in the third person, contrasting with such stories as 'A Country House', where the first-person narrative is a defining feature of the writing. Other techniques, however, are not only retained but developed. The repetition of key words or phrases, for example, occurs extensively in *Winter Sonata*, as does the use of musical references. Edwards's use of musical terms throughout the text reinforces the sense of the novel's musical composition: Olivia finds that 'time seemed to move for her so slowly, like a long *adagio*' (*WS*, 182); while for Premiss the trees and the sky 'had an air of restrained gaiety like a little scherzo in a minor key' (*WS*, 76); and Nettle has a dream that returns to him 'like a chord of music' (*WS*, 71). But the influence of music pervades the novel not only in a symbolic but also in a structural fashion.[22] Images or motifs – Olivia's 'large, sad eyes' (and, in fact, eyes in general), the branches of the trees, the moon, white flowers – accrue significance as they are repeated. Scenes also recur: Nettle, for example, reflects on his first meeting with Olivia several times throughout the novel. Such repetition is a key characteristic of the sonata:

> The organization of the sonata is partly effected by recurrence of phrase – that is, by the employment, at a later period, of musical sentences or paragraphs which have already been presented earlier in the work, and which are recognized by the hearer on their re-appearance.[23]

The set pattern of Nettle's life, his daily walk to the post office, his weekly visit to his uncle's home and the intermittent invitations to the Neran and Curle household, serve to add a sense of ritual and rigid form. This sense of repetitive and cyclical temporal structure pervades the text as a whole; although it encompasses a period of some months, it begins with the dawn of a new morning and ends with the onset of night. '[I]f a tune is to leave us with any impression of coherence it must end in the same key in which it began', claims W. H. Hadow, which is precisely what Edwards does in *Winter Sonata*.[24] Like the stories in *Rhapsody*, the narrative of *Winter Sonata* lacks the climax or conclusion integral to the traditional Victorian novel: there are no marriage proposals, no deaths and no revelations to offer closure. *Winter Sonata* ends very much in the tone in which it began. The opening section focused on Nettle's arrival in the village on the last day before winter came when he was full of hope that here, unlike in town, he would manage to remain well through-out the winter. At the end of the novel again there is a sense of hope: Nettle, though he has not managed to avoid illness, is recovering well, and a new moon is shining down on him as he leaves the Nerans' house.

Such moments of optimism, however, are few and far between in *Winter Sonata*. The overwhelming impression that remains after reading the novel is that of lassitude, of hibernation, of lives half-lived. Edwards's characters suffer from loneliness as well as various forms of debilitating depression, like that which was increasingly coming to dominate Edwards's own life. Nettle is isolated and longs to be a part of a world from which he is excluded; Olivia suffers from lethargy and depression that she conceals from her family; George is desperately lacking self-worth; Pauline Clark aches for loving attention and comfort, but receives scorn and abuse instead. Even Premiss is an isolated man: he puts on a charismatic front when in company, but he dislikes being alone at night and suffers from insomnia. The various mental and emotional illnesses that the characters experience serve to slow down the novel's tempo. Nettle's illness overshadows the second and third movements of the novel; Olivia's increasing depression and Premiss's insomnia, coupled with the repetition of words such as 'tired' and 'depressed' and their derivatives, all serve to sustain a sense of lives subdued, as nature is subdued in winter. And yet, when she was writing the novel, Edwards was apparently unaware of the isolated positions in which she placed her characters. A letter to David Garnett, follow-ing a visit to him in 1931, shows her reaction when re-reading her own work; the chill of it struck her as if for the first time:

> When I got home, first of all I read *Winter Sonata* to see if anything in it justified all the kindness people had shown me, and I must confess that I could hardly read through it . . . it is so bleak and cold that I nearly got frostbite while I read, and the chief thing it portrays is an awful emptiness, very distressing to have to read about.[25]

The appearance of *Winter Sonata* in 1928 signalled a pause in Edwards's creative writing career. During the period following its publication,

Edwards's home life became increasingly difficult and her depression spiralled. She was not to see any more of her fiction in print during her lifetime.

A Welsh Cinderella in Bloomsbury: power dynamics and cultural colonialism

Winter Sonata and *Rhapsody* had gained Edwards many admirers. Literary critic Gerald Gould wrote in a review of *Rhapsody* 'Miss Dorothy Edwards is an exciting writer',[1] while novelist Arnold Bennett referred to her as a writer of genius.[2] Recommended with avidity in London literary circles, *Rhapsody* caught the attention of David Garnett, a well-established author and member of the avant-garde Bloomsbury group, who recalls in his autobiography *The Familiar Faces*:

> In 1927, when I was still flushed with success as a writer . . . Raymond Mortimer thought I ought to read a new book *Rhapsody* by an unknown writer Dorothy Edwards. I bought a copy and read it. Raymond was right. The stories were peculiarly to my taste and, what is more, revealed an entirely original talent. I was greatly excited by them, and wrote to the authoress.[3]

Garnett's admiration only increased on reading *Winter Sonata*, and he wrote to Edwards:

> In *Winter Sonata* you have shown that you are a great writer & an absolutely original one: your field is fairly small, but in literature & poetry, unlike architecture, size is of no account . . . you have done something absolutely new, and after reading you all living novelists have sunk in my estimation, much as though with the book you had created a new scale of values . . . *Winter Sonata* is one of the few great novels in English literature – and its [*sic*] amusing to think of it getting in beside the other immortal novels some of whom have been snoring,

sound asleep for a century or two, others spitting in the corners of the carriage, and one or two fat ones taking up more than their share of the seats. *Winter Sonata* will be rather quiet, shy at being put in the first-class carriage, and then a good deal amused when she identifies the odd company in which she finds herself.[4]

'Did I tell you that I had a wonderful letter from David Garnett? He liked *Winter Sonata* apparently very much & he seems to be an altogether charming person', Edwards wrote to Beryl Jones in 1929 on receiving Garnett's letter.[5] Edwards's reply to him is congenial:

it is not only pleasure that your letter gives me but really a kind of guarantee of succeeding. And then I will not decline a seat in the first-class carriage if it is offered to me, but I shall help you make one or two of the fat passengers move up a bit.[6]

With his reference to a first-class carriage, Garnett couches his response to Edwards's work in terms of social difference. But her reply that she will 'not decline a seat in the first-class carriage . . . but . . . make one or two of the fat passengers move up a bit', reflects her refusal to comply with hierarchical social systems and is prescient of the tone that her future relationship with Garnett would take. The nature of those power relations which Edwards investigated in her fiction became exemplified in her relationship with Garnett, as she experienced at first hand an encounter with the type of dominant powers that she had earlier dissected in her fiction.

Garnett and Edwards arranged to meet at the Nonesuch Press Office in Great James Street, London, in January 1929. '[I] shall appear very agitated & excited at meeting you, so you will recognize me easily', Garnett wrote in a letter to her beforehand.[7] His recollection of their meeting, however, shows him to have been somewhat disenchanted. 'There was a ring at the bell. I opened the door and there stood a girl, rather stumpy in an Italian grey-green Bersaglieri officer's cloak, fresh-complexioned, with protruding front teeth, eager, ardent, embarrassed, shy', he recalls.[8] Although his admiration of Edwards's writing, and her intellect and intelligence (traits that Garnett found to be 'rare in a woman')[9] is evident, his account of their first meeting indicates that Edwards's physical appearance had a strong effect on his response to her, and he later describes her as:

> short and rather fat, with a buxom low-breasted figure which was not improved by her square-cut low-necked, clumsy home-made dresses and her lack of any form of corset or brassiere . . . her beauty . . . spoilt by prominent, protruding upper teeth which were not only ugly in themselves, but spoilt what might have otherwise been pretty lips.[10]

Despite Garnett's disappointment at Edwards's rather unglamorous appearance, the pair hit it off immediately. Garnett was eager to introduce Edwards, whom he dubbed his 'Welsh Cinderella', to literary society, his 'great world of well-known people'.[11] Early on in their acquaintance he wrote to inform her that

> On Thursday night I've been asked to a small party after dinner – all the people are admirers of yours I think – I was asked to bring you but said we probably wouldn't come – if you would like new faces after a long journey we would, after all, go.[12]

Evidently aware of the valuable nature of praise bestowed on her by someone in Garnett's position, Edwards received Garnett's efforts positively; after their first meeting she wrote to Beryl Jones saying,

> He has offered to help, even to take charge of the business-side of my writing. He thinks I ought to make a certain amount of money & says that one ought to write as little as possible & see that one gets paid enormous prices for what one does write . . . He betrayed the utmost anxiety to be the person to introduce me to literary London . . . I am excited and thrilled at the thought of staying with him & at the party. I hope he doesn't change his mind.[13]

The after-dinner party was soon followed by a tea party at Vanessa Bell's home, and a soirée at Duncan Grant's studio, where she was introduced to Virginia Woolf and Lytton Strachey.[14] Invitations to the Garnetts' Cambridgeshire country home, Hilton Hall, were received thick and fast during 1929–30, when Edwards and Garnett's wife, Ray, also struck up a friendship. During a Whitsun break spent at Hilton Hall, Edwards met editor John Hayward, mathematician Frank Ramsey and Alec Penrose; on another trip, this time to Hamspray House, the home that Strachey shared with artist Dora Carrington, she met painter Henry Lamb and fellow Welshman, Augustus John. 'O Duw, there's nice he was! I realised what a strain Englishes are, when I was there', she wrote to Jones and Kelly of her meeting with John.[15] Carrington was delighted with her 'favourite',[16] and wrote to Edwards saying

> Its [sic] difficult to tell you how much I loved your books. I read them more often than any book except Wuthering Heights – I never believed you would come here. I still find it difficult to believe anything I wanted so much, could have come true.[17]

While Edwards evidently appreciated Garnett's enthusiastic friendship and recognition of her literary talent, it is apparent from her letters to Jones and Kelly that, with his friends, Edwards felt uncomfortably out of place:

> I went to a swell party the other night full of beautiful females in long frocks with no backs to them, & distinguished & irresponsible-looking young men, and when I wasn't gazing at David, I was shyly attempting to give the right answers when several of the beautiful females dropped onto their knees at my feet & assured me in various ways that they were passionate admirers of my work. I should have succeeded better had I not been controlling an impulse to tell them not to sit on the floor in such nice clothes.[18]

Perhaps her sense of displacement is hardly surprising: while the Bloomsbury group was considered to provide an alternative voice to the stereotypical English ruling class, their exclusive nature has been extensively chronicled, even by those within the circle. Frances Partridge, Ray Garnett's sister, for example, commented in her 1981 volume *Memories* that:

Bloomsburies called spades spades and said what they thought; they didn't keep afloat in a social atmosphere by the wing-flapping of small talk – if they were bored by the conversation they showed it. This disconcerted the unconfident and gave them a justified reputation for rudeness, nor do I think it any more admirable now than I found it then; but they could nearly all of them be extraordinarily kind at times, *if they liked you*.[19]

On his part, Garnett relished his patronage of Edwards:

Though Ray and I did not seem rich to ourselves, and seemed poor to most of our friends, to Dorothy we represented the bourgeoisie, able to enjoy luxuries. We were also her only link with the great world of well-known people. Thus we were able to give her experiences that she could not otherwise have come by. She had always been extremely poor . . . In our company she could enjoy a glass of wine, a drive in a private car, or a seat in the pit at the theatre.[20]

But Edwards's reaction to his circle of friends did not give Garnett the gratification that he had anticipated, as he observes in his autobiography:

One of the pleasures of adopting a Welsh Cinderella as one's sister is in introducing her to the world. Naturally if Cinderella is a talented writer, the pleasure is all the greater. I anticipated, therefore, a good deal of pleasure of this sort from taking Dorothy to a party at Duncan's studio at which both Lytton Strachey and Virginia Woolf were to be present and Dorothy on her part was overjoyed at the prospect of meeting them as she greatly admired their books . . . I did my part with right goodwill. I introduced Dorothy to Lytton Strachey who had read *Rhapsody* and made it plain in a few murmurs that he had done so . . . Then I introduced her to Virginia Woolf who seemed vague but full of friendly astonishment . . . But presently the literary lions drifted away and there was Dorothy flushed and holding forth. We stayed till the end of the party and . . . I asked Dorothy how she had liked it . . . What I wanted were her impressions of Lytton Strachey and Virginia Woolf, but I got none . . . her impressions of Lytton and Virginia and indeed of Duncan Grant, Clive Bell, Roger Fry and Vanessa Bell were precisely nil. She had noticed nobody, had observed nothing.[21]

Edwards's letters to Jones and Kelly, however, are full of astute comments on the people she encountered while under Garnett's patronage. Virginia Woolf is described as 'a steel greyhound, swift enough to be gentle. I loved her';[22] Vanessa Bell as 'an exceedingly beautiful absent-minded lady of about 50 . . . who finding herself sitting at dinner next to Mr Asquith, vaguely connecting him with the subject, asked him kindly if he were interested in politics'.[23] Lytton Strachey she describes as 'absolutely charming . . . He gives one the impression of immense kindness & an affectionate disposition.'[24] Letters from this period suggest that Edwards felt Garnett's need for affirmation keenly, but deliberately withheld her observations from him. Of a forthcoming holiday to be spent with Ray Garnett, for example, Edwards says to Kelly and Jones:

I have rather reluctantly accepted an invitation to stay with Ray Garnett in the village where Theodore Powys lives. She has been lent a cottage there for a week . . . I go because it is quite clear that David is dying to know what effect Powys will have on me – & this rather rouses my curiosity. 'You will love him, everyone loves Theo', they assure me – . I feel sure, on the other hand that I shall not love him, & even that it will tax my Christian spirit heavily to like him, but we shall see.[25]

While Garnett's patronage of Edwards was evidently well intended, his account of Edwards in his autobiographical *The Familiar Faces* reflects a rather distorted understanding of Edwards's background and upbringing in line with that fitting for his parochial dependent, his Welsh Cinderella.[26] Describing Edward Edwards as 'a poor schoolmaster in a Welsh village', Garnett recounts a simplified and romantic view of Edwards's upbringing that is in fact a far cry from the life that the Edwards family led in a heavily industrialized and largely Anglicized valley, and where the Edwards family maintained a comfortable lifestyle in comparison to that of their neighbours.[27] Stephen Knight goes as far as to argue that Garnett's introduction of Edwards to London literary society was in itself a colonial act. '[T]he self-indulgent promoting by David Garnett of the brilliant and tragic Dorothy Edwards in the inherently hostile Bloomsbury group' is, he says, 'characteristic . . . of the encounter between colonizing power and colonized writers.'[28]

The lifestyle maintained by Garnett was, of course, not altogether different from the privileged existence that Edwards depicted, and criticized, in her fiction. Her association with Garnett and his friends gave Edwards a first-hand view of this mode of living which she would not have experienced to the same extent in south Wales. As her contact with Garnett and his circle increased, so did her awareness of the role of grateful parochial dependent in which she had been cast. In correspondence with Jones and Kelly, she is acerbic:

> Mother thinks that contact with these nobs sells my books – though there is no evidence of this at all . . . It seems rather awful strenuously to avoid my friends for the sake of working, & then go eagerly to stay with my hereditary enemies. However you understand why I do this, & how much of an ordeal by ice it is for me to mix with these Englishes.[29]

This letter suggests that her trips to England allowed her in part to act as a sort of socialist Welsh spy, gathering crucial material with which to continue to attack the ruling classes in her writing. Later she writes:

> I am still baffled and intimidated by the English spirit, though I now believe myself to be on its track. I have some clues which may turn out to be valuable, but so far no arrests have been made . . . I shall be very glad to come back to you when this pilgrimage is over.[30]

At this time, Edwards became more strongly aware of her Welsh identity and of her class status, perhaps in reaction to the affluent English society that she encountered, which not only heightened her sense of displacement but fuelled her interest in the Welsh nationalist movement. After returning to Cardiff from a London visit, she tells Beryl Jones,

> It is awfully queer to be home again. It is like cutting a hole in a beautiful coloured not very meaningful canvas and slipping behind it to a dull

dingy sordid existence full, comparatively, of struggle & hatred, in which however one is conscious of a great depth of feeling. I am trying to see Wales & Welshies with new eyes and I see lots of queer things I hadn't noticed before . . . It is awfully hard for me to believe that all the nice Englishes I have met are now saying malicious things about me to enquirers but so it must be since they do it to each other.[31]

By the late 1920s, Edwards was taking Welsh-language lessons from Gwenda Gruffydd, fellow Rhiwbina resident and wife of Cardiff academic W. J. Gruffydd. 'I have learnt Welsh for five months & am under no illusion about my knowing it', she says.[32] This did little to deter her from becoming concerned with political events taking place in Wales. '"Sympathy with Welsh aspirations is the main thing," she used to say', recalled Harold Watkins, and to the surprise of friends and acquaintances Edwards was soon adding Welsh nationalist to her ever-increasing list of identities.[33] In a 1930 letter to Saunders Lewis, held at the National Library of Wales and quoted by Katie Gramich in her comparative article on Edwards and Welsh-language writer Kate Roberts, Edwards indicates her growing passion for Plaid Cymru's aims:

May I repeat my congratulations on your speech last night. I was brought up on the Red Flag in the days when it was very red, and I never permit myself to be carried away at a political meeting by anything less than a promise of the kingdom of heaven on earth, so I am saying something that I mean very deeply when I say that I was completely carried away by the sincerity the genuine imaginative depth and the courageous and firm grasp of the exact, present state of life in Wales in its very fullest sense, which you showed last night. Whether you get in or not – and I hope from my heart that you do – you have already shown the point from which action and enthusiasm must take off, and from this something is bound to come.[34]

By the 1930s, her letters to Jones and Kelly became increasingly peppered with national references, and wider experience of the Bloomsbury set did not leave her feeling more at home with them. She found herself alienated, partly as a result of her lack of funds and her sense of ethnic difference, but also because of her difficulty in reading their social conventions:

I behave very badly at parties. I speak to people I don't know & get snubbed; then I in all simplicity snub the next kind soul who speaks to me, because I think that is what they like. It is partly because I know I am badly dressed & I am too vain to hide behind anyone if David [Garnett] isn't there. And it is partly nationalism – that divider of human beings – or rather that reasonable accepter of division that could be bridged.[35]

In this letter, Edwards is working out her ideas concerning nationalism quite literally on the page: first, it is a 'divider of human beings', then clarified as a 'division' that can be 'bridged', evoking nationalism in terms of a patriotic pride rather than aggressive nation-building, and is indicative of her move towards a more patriotic form of socialism.

In an early letter to Garnett dated 27 November 1928, Edwards demonstrates an acute awareness of the burden of literary obligation she feels Wales casts upon its writers, saying: 'You must know that every Welshman who has learnt to hold a pen believes himself to be a future novelist that my country has been some what dubiously expecting for a century. So I too believe this.'[36] Garnett's response to Edwards's nationality is reflective of many of the tensions outlined above. In his autobiography, he describes his response on first reading Edwards's work in the light of her nationality: 'I was a good deal interested in the way in which she had carefully avoided giving a hint of Welsh local colour or Welsh sentiment in any of her stories', he says.[37] He apparently expected Edwards to offer a certain parochial view of her homeland, and this is evident in his response to her throughout their relationship, from his choice of ethnically based nickname (Welsh Cinderella) to his suggestions for her writing (he requests from her a 'Welsh sketch of narrow valleys'[38]). In his autobiography, Garnett claims that Edwards's first letter to him 'seems almost intended to give the impression that its writer was a Welsh speaker who thought in that language . . . Later I learned that she knew French, German, Italian, Latin and Greek – but hardly any Welsh.'[39] The comment made by Edwards that so misled Garnett was:

1 Dorothy Edwards aged 9, 1913. The text on the verso of this photograph reads 'With love to Mama from Dorothy for her Birthday. May
13 1913.' Reproduced with kind permission of Richard Garnett and
Charles Deering McCormick Library of Special Collections, Northwestern University Library.

2 Edward Edwards's gravestone. The inscription reads: 'This book was laid by the Tynewydd Ward Labour Party, the Trade Unions & the Cooperative Society. In memory of Edward Edwards, Schoolmaster & Socialist Pioneer.'

3 Dorothy Edwards and David Garnett (*c*.1930) at Hamspray House. Reproduced with kind permission of Gill Coleridge of Rogers, Coleridge and White, and King's College Library, Cambridge.

4 Dorothy Edwards (*c*.1930) at Hamspray House. Reproduced with kind
   permission of Gill Coleridge of Rogers, Coleridge and White, and King's
   College Library, Cambridge.

It seems to me that I am still wrestling with the possibility – or indeed it may be the ultimate impossibility – of finding a way of expressing in the English language something that seems quite alien to everything that language has been created and moulded to express.[40]

Far from desiring to give a false impression regarding her linguistic abilities, Edwards's comment (and the effect that it had on Garnett) demonstrates, for those familiar with the colonial nature of language in Wales at least, an awareness of the complexity of language politics. In fact, the particular linguistic history and make-up of the industrial area where Edwards was born and raised meant that the 'English' spoken in these areas at this time would have been strongly marked by Welsh, in terms of accent and grammatical features as well as by the use of some Welsh-language expressions. Edwards's comment is suggestive of the difficulties experienced by a society that faces the task of interpreting the cultural, social and historical nuances of their heritage in a language other than their own, first language or not.[41]

By 1930, the relationship between Garnett and Edwards was faltering and, two years after their first meeting, contact lapsed between the pair. Then, in January 1931, Garnett wrote to Edwards lamenting the loss of her friendship. 'I long to see you. I long to hear from you; please let it be good news that you have written something & approve of it', he wrote.[42] In order to prevent such a silence between them again, in this letter Garnett proposes that he and Edwards adopt one another as brother and sister. '[H]owever much we neglected each other & quarrelled we should always be tied by something which could not be got rid of', he explained to her.[43] Edwards readily accepted Garnett's suggestion, but correspondence between the two was apparently sporadic in 1931 and 1932, and there is little evidence that she visited Garnett as much as she had in the late 1920s, if in fact at all. Edwards's developing preoccupation with national identity, in addition to her class views, became both a source of stimulating debate and a bone of contention for both parties. As her awareness of her national difference in the face of English identity developed, she wrote to Garnett in 1932:

I no longer blanch when someone says I ought to write in Welsh, I no longer smirk when someone says what fine people we are and in a month or two I expect to be able to give anyone who says anything really disagreeable about Wales a sock on the jaw.[44]

The renewed correspondence offered precious reprieve to Edwards. During the period following the publication of *Rhapsody* and *Winter Sonata*, her life had become dominated by domestic struggle and unhappiness. Her anxieties about her mother, her money-earning powers and the lack of progress of her writing had only increased since the 1920s, and the depression that had reared its head during her post-university years became increasingly crippling. In one letter to Jones and Kelly, written during this period, she wrote: 'I can feel another attack of depression coming on. If it is worse than the last, heaven help me.'[45] In another, written in *c*.1932–3, she is more explicit, saying: 'I am discovering a few things about Wales which one only discovers when one has been on the verge of suicide in a country.'[46] Her descriptions of the physical effects that this depression had on her are unnerving to read and must have caused Jones and Kelly, her closest confidantes, some anguish. In a letter to Kelly she says:

I dont [sic] really quite know what is the matter with me. I feel about my mind what people must feel about their bodies when they are drunk. It works in much the same way as usual but I am damned if I know who is moving it, it aint [sic] me. This may be a direct revelation of God, only I haven't recognized it. I can neither plan nor see ahead, and I can't even worry about it in a reasonable and human manner. I just get these appalling fits of absolute unbearable depression which however don't last very long now.[47]

Her guilt over her mother's illness and her resentment of her carer role left Edwards feeling deeply troubled. 'Mother keeps on being ill. She comes in from town crying because she can't walk. I don't know what to do', she wrote to Kelly and Jones in despair, for Vida's Christian Science beliefs led her to refuse any medical care.[48] In a letter to Sona Rosa Burstein, Edwards indicates that the difficulties of her situation at home were not only exacerbating her depressive state, but making it impossible for her to write:

> This is what I am feeling. My mother is really ill – her hand shakes all the time with rheumatism & her leg is beginning to drag when she walks. She cries & complains & has visions of a depressing future when she can't move. Meanwhile I have to take over the housework. There isn't really much but she won't take her meals regularly and she won't let me manage the house at all. She holds the reins & I get blamed if the horses take the wrong turning . . . There is not a single moment during the day except when she is out when I am sure of not being interrupted though of course I don't actually get interrupted all the time. But it is as much as I can do to get anything done, I get depressed & nervy & restless. I feel I ought to be detached enough not to mind being treated like this by a poor woman who is in pain but the constant complaints against everything & everybody give me a picture of the world which depresses me to the point of suicide. It is quite impossible for me to believe that I shall ever write anything again.[49]

The financial implications of Edwards's freelance status contributed extensively to the tension between mother and daughter. Their meagre income, consisting mainly of Edward Edwards's pension, was supplemented by the small and unreliable wages that Edwards earned by reviewing books for the *Western Mail and South Wales News* and some extra-mural teaching at University College of South Wales and Monmouthshire.[50] When Jones and Kelly sent Edwards a cheque as a birthday gift, she wrote in reply,

> As a matter of fact the very sight of money in this benighted household at this moment rather relieves the tension. I think it wouldn't be a bad thing if I framed it & hung it over the mantelpiece to reassure mother . . . [who] wilts before the gaze of the bank clerk every time she cashes a cheque.[51]

There were reprieves – odd weeks snatched with Jones and Kelly – but in Rhiwbina Edwards found little escape from the drudgery of her everyday life. With their correspondence re-established, Garnett too became a confidante with whom Edwards could discuss her home situation. A letter that Edwards sent to him on 9 October 1932 indicates the extreme emotional stress that she was suffering: 'I contemplate easy ways of slipping out of this world of tears . . . last week I nearly did it.'[52] Obviously affected by his friend's distressed tone, Garnett devised a means to provide Edwards with a haven in which to write. He invited her to live in the attic of the Endsleigh Street flat that he shared with his family where, in exchange for board and lodging and peace in which to write, Edwards would act as a live-in babysitter for their youngest son, William.[53]

Desperate to escape from the tension at home, and frustrated over the lack of progress in her writing, Edwards's excitement and relief at Garnett's offer are evident in a letter to Jones and Kelly:

> [W]hen things had got so bad here that I had really given up hope of ever writing anything again because I have become so nauseatingly bored with everything here although I am so fond of Wales, when I had began to look and worse still to dress like a poor companion, and to read books of travel with a wistful & hopeless expression of envy on my countenance, suddenly David Garnett presents me with an attic to starve in in London & Mother says she will have a companion to look after her & I can go next month. I shall have to keep myself & pay the companion's wages otherwise I shall be free. Garnett says, & _means_ that he will throw me out if I don't write something good immediately . . . this adventure . . . may not turn out to be nice. But if you could only imagine how awful this year has been! She [Vida] is really very ill by now & needs incessant attention which even on the days when I have the best will in the world, I absolutely forget to give her. So I think she is glad secretly that she is to have someone to look after her at last properly.[54]

The move to London appeared to mark a new positive chapter in Edwards's life: she would be in a lively city with a flourishing literary atmosphere and with friends who understood and empathized with the problems that a writer faced. 'I will hardly know what has happened when I get peace to work & to read. I am going to live on cold water & salad & type all day . . . I must plunge into work', she wrote to Jones.[55] But at the same time she makes a disturbingly prophetic comment: 'If my attic proves to have been a vain dream & I have to stay at home instead I shall put my head in the gas oven & turn on the tap.'[56]

Edwards moved to London in January 1933.[57] 'I am very happy here, my attic continues to be nice & I would love to be having you to tea this afternoon', she wrote in her ever-faithful correspondence with Jones and Kelly.[58] But her optimistic tone quickly faded as she became disheartened by her lack of progress with her writing and frustrated with her relative poverty:

> Life here instead of being all beer & skittles as I was expecting has been rather difficult & drab after all.
>
> I find London too big & dirty, I couldn't get to work at all first & now though I am working & have turned out a few decent things, I have rather a guilty conscience & Garnett spends a lot of his spare time manufacturing excuses for me . . . I live like a hermit & wrestle with my muse. I have awfully little money (but I don't want to borrow any). I want to see what it is like to feel that one has none . . . I have given up theatres & operas because I haven't any money . . . I have earned practically nothing so I am still not my own master.[59]

Edwards struggled under the constant pressure of having to please her benefactor and become once again the talented but dependent Welsh Cinderella: 'I have just begun my novel – no more. I <u>must</u> get it finished before I get home . . . I dare not look Garnett in the face if I don't get my novel written before I leave here', she wrote to Jones and Kelly.[60]

Meanwhile, Cardiff friends were becoming concerned for her welfare in London. Harold Watkins recalls:

> [T]he poor girl was having a very thin time. A friend of mine who took her out to dinner occasionally when he was in London gave me the impression that she was not even having enough to eat . . . she had lost much of her natural vivacity.[61]

Her letters to Jones and Kelly substantiate Watkins's suspicions: 'I am in disgrace & rags. You will not recognize me. I have not finished my novel & I have no clothes . . . I hate hate hate London', she says.[62]

At one point she ran out of money completely, writing a frantic plea to Jones and Kelly to 'send . . . 10/- as soon as possible'.[63] Back home in Pen-y-dre the new arrangement was not running as smoothly as Edwards may have hoped and, during her stay in London, Vida changed companions no less than three times. Edwards's guilt on leaving her mother is evident: 'it isn't easy for her to have to make a big change like this now', she writes defensively.[64] In another: 'It's partly my fault since I trained her into habits that no companion could possibly fit into.'[65]

It was inevitable that Edwards would find it difficult to live as a quasi-equal alongside the Bloomsbury set, with their financially independent lifestyle. Not Bloomsbury by virtue of his family or his education, Garnett claims in his autobiography that he and his wife were 'poor' in comparison to their circle and, during this difficult period, he did all he could to help Edwards while allowing her to maintain some independence.[66] 'I tried to help her to earn a little money by giving her books to review – which she was completely unable to do', he claimed.[67] In the face of Edwards's poverty, Garnett became increasingly defensive and antagonistic. Her socialist views he dismissed as 'emotional and . . . divorced from reality', maintained only by a sense of filial duty.[68] He apparently became increasingly aware of, and uncomfortable with, her censure of the lifestyle maintained by him and his friends, a censure grounded in the socialist beliefs that she still held. He says: '[Dorothy] disapproved of Ray and me increasingly and showed that she did. Her disapproval was political and social – we were well-fed, we were not working for the Revolution, we ate meat.'[69]

Evidently, Edwards's occupation of the attic room at Endsleigh Street was becoming increasingly difficult for both parties. But, despite the fact that Edwards's friendship with Garnett was beginning to break down, she had begun to write again: she describes herself to Jones and Kelly as 'partially revived',[70] saying 'my Muse has awakened but I don't know if I can keep up with him'.[71] Edwards showed her new work to her publisher, Wishart, and was offered a contract for a new volume of short stories.[72] But Garnett was unimpressed with her new writing:

> She brought me her stories – there were three of them, all somehow on the same model, breathing the same breath . . . Each one was unmistakably the work of Dorothy Edwards – but each was unsatisfactory, incompletely realised, inferior . . . The author was never there when we met to discuss them.[73]

While Edwards's writing progressed slowly, her mental state deteriorated rapidly, as is evident from the diary that she began to keep in August 1933, lovingly addressed directly to a friend and contemporary of her father, Stitt Wilson, who lived in the US with his wife.[74] In her diary entries, her mood swings from the euphoric to the despondent. 'It seems as though everything in me has by now died once', she writes in an entry for 10 August 1933.[75] But, equally, in this diary there is a suggestion of renewed hope: Edwards begins to be excited by her writing again. In fact, she becomes uncharacteristically hopeful – another entry reads:

> I really have begun a new life, I am happy again after many years of disturbance and fear and lostness; I even feel that there is in me a new power of some kind, or rather an old power reawakened that I can now use.[76]

At the time of writing, Edwards met and fell in love with Ronald Harding, a young cellist in a London quartet, whom Edwards described to Jones and Kelly as 'adorably Welsh'.[77] 'He has been very good to me in these few weeks that I have known him. He has given me back a feeling of my own right to exist', she wrote in her diary.[78] The potential of a close and genuine contact with another evidently gave Edwards a renewed vigour for life, and demonstrated a move away from her penchant for casting potential lovers in a mentor or father-figure role, established with her engagement to John Thorburn and perpetuated in her relations with Garnett and Stitt Wilson.

Perhaps the relationship with Harding had inspired Edwards to create one of the few positive partnerships in her fiction. 'The Problem of Life' (the very title of which is telling in the context of Edwards's mental state at this time) was composed in Endsleigh Street in 1933. In this story, a middle-aged man, Mr Rose, visits his friend Mr Barron's countryside home, where he lives with his half-siblings, Adrian and Rachel. Adrian is a sensitive student who reads avidly and, despite his close relationship with his sister, feels very isolated. During a dinner party in the company of Rose, Barron, Rachel and their neighbours Mrs Chenery and her daughter Emilia, Adrian suffers from a fit of depression not unlike those described by Edwards in her letters to Jones and Kelly:

> Adrian was very conscious of this feeling of being shut in, but it was something he sometimes experienced. It came inexplicably and went again; it brought with it a kind of melancholy somewhere deep down in his soul, too far down for him to find it and cast it away. And he felt this now. (*R*, 259)

Emilia has the insight and sensitivity to pick up on Adrian's despondent mood: 'I looked at you once during dinner and I thought then that you felt sad inside', she says to him (*R*, 260). Adrian is 'so much astonished at this that he did not answer', but from this point on, the two are able to confide in one another about the depression that they apparently share (*R*, 261). Emilia, in her sympathetic understanding of his feelings, pulls Adrian back from the brink of isolation.

But, for Edwards, in the end, there was no one to pull her back from the brink. Harding was married, and the short-lived affair was called off. She tells Jones and Kelly:

> I really fell in love with Harding . . . We decided to join forces & went gaily on, I planning the kind of ménage we should have, & he planning the details of separating from his wife, & then suddenly we found ourselves up against the rotten Puritanism of our benighted country. For he would, it seems, most certainly be thrown out of the orchestra, though he is the best person in it, if we lived in sin in the sight of all Cardiff. And since neither of us feel like meeting in a back street, and neither of us are sure enough of our careers at this moment to throw everything over and risk it, we parted sorrowfully.[79]

By the time the split with Harding came, relations between Edwards and Garnett had broken down completely and, in December 1933, she left Endsleigh Street suddenly. According to various newspapers, she returned to Cardiff with the intention of writing her new collection of short stories in 'a bungalow in Marshfield'.[80] Despite the temporary nature of her arrangement with Garnett, Edwards had seen the move as her long-awaited break from home and its incumbent responsibilities: 'I don't intend of course having at last got away from home to go back there if there is any sort of alternative', she had told Jones and Kelly on first moving to London.[81] Apparently, no alternative was available and, within a fortnight of returning to the Pen-y-dre home that she shared with her mother, Edwards threw herself under a train. She was thirty-one years old. Tellingly, in one of the last letters that Edwards wrote to Jones and Kelly, Edwards said: 'I don't sing now. Me [sic] music is stilled.'[82]

On the day of her death, Edwards had spent the morning burning some papers in the garden, but when she left the house Vida noticed nothing unusual in her demeanour or actions. It is reasonable to assume that the documents she burned included letters from her former fiancé, John Thorburn, and her 'bad novel', which she had requested Beryl Jones to destroy if she were to die suddenly. On the evening of Friday 5 January 1934 Edwards left home to take a walk on Rhiwbina Hill, during which she called on her friends Mr and Mrs Tom Russell, with whom she shared her passion for music. The Russells, like Vida, noticed nothing out of the ordinary in her manner or conversation. At 9.30 p.m. that evening a Mr Rich of Caerphilly was on his way to work when he noticed a young woman matching Edwards's description rush past him and head towards the nearby railway line. At 7.20 a.m. the next morning Edwards's body was found on the track: she had died as a result of a fracture at the base of the skull caused by an engine, probably belonging to a train that had passed at 10.34 p.m. on the Friday night. A note found in her pocket read: 'I am killing myself because I have never sincerely loved any human being all my life. I have accepted kindness and friendship and even love without gratitude, and given nothing in return.'[83]

This note led the coroner to conclude the inquest into her death with a verdict of suicide while in a state of unsound mind.[84] A close study of Edwards's fiction reveals that she had worked out the sentiments expressed in her suicide note some time before her death. In *Winter Sonata*, after George Curle has found his cousin Eleanor Neran crying over some throwaway comment made by their house-guest, David Premiss, he thinks it 'really extraordinary' that Eleanor 'should cry because someone had told her that she was incapable of love' (*WS*, 175). Of course, it is not in the least surprising that Eleanor should be upset to be deemed incapable of experiencing such a principal human emotion. But the most striking similarity occurs with Richard's comment to Mary in 'La Penseuse', the evening before he embarks for his trip to Italy. 'I suppose there are girls like you . . . You take my love and live on it . . . and give nothing in return', he accuses her (*R*, 202).[85] And yet, ironically, in Edwards's fictions it is women, like Mary in 'La Penseuse', Olivia Neran in *Winter Sonata* and Leonora Morn in 'Days', who suffer as a result of such cold and unloving treatment at the hands of men.

Edwards's suicide inevitably left her friends and family shattered, particularly her by now elderly and invalid mother, on whom this note must have had a particularly devastating effect. 'This has been a terrible shock . . . [Dorothy] was quite happy all the time she was home and full of her work', Vida wrote to Garnett of her daughter on 12 January 1934.[86] In another letter she describes herself, understandably, as 'heartbroken'.[87] Vida died just six months later, on 29 October 1934, aged sixty-eight.[88]

Excluded by language from the Welsh intelligentsia, excluded by nationality and class from the English bourgeoisie, excluded by gender and education from the working-class communities to which her politics, and ultimately her heart, belonged, Edwards's attempt to negotiate a liminal space in which to develop her life and work failed with devastating consequences. And yet, in the period leading up to her suicide, Edwards produced some of her most fascinating short stories. The vantage point that she had gained as a Welsh woman living in the English capital added new concern to her fiction, ideas which she had held, in theory, for some time. Edwards's association with Garnett and his Bloomsbury crowd saw her, perhaps as a result of being confronted with her Welsh difference in a very real way, become increasingly concerned with issues of national identity and colonial politics, and their relationship with class and gender tensions. The stories 'Mutiny' and the until recently unpublished 'Mitter', both written in 1933 when she was living in the attic of Garnett's Endsleigh Street flat, show Edwards taking a step closer to understanding the complex nature of the gendered, class-based and imperialist nature of the power structures that dominated her society that she had first invoked in her story 'The Conquered' in 1926. In these stories, Edwards demonstrates an intense awareness of the historical subjugation of her country and its parallel with other oppressed nations, and as such her work constitutes a specifically Welsh form of postcolonial writing.

During her time in exile in London, Edwards became more overtly self-reflective in her writings: her 1933 journal contains recollections of Ogmore Vale and of her father, the only explicit examples of autobiographical writing found so far in her work. Here, she gives an indication of her political outlook at this time as well as recording some particularly important incidents from her childhood. In one entry, for example, she writes: 'I hate Winston Churchill & the British Empire, & I like anyone who is really suffering from any injustice, political or social.'[89] In a further diary entry, she recalls in some detail her father's behaviour during the early years of her life. Each year as the summer vacation approached, Edwards would notice a 'subtle change' in her father as he prepared for their family holiday, during which he carried out rather un-conventional experiments:

No sooner had we crossed the border into England on our way to some south coast resort than there was no longer any doubt about it, he had turned into a Frenchman. And in a broken English that contained every odd pun or quaintness made by any Frenchman up to that date, throughout the holiday he would seek encounters with the native English and so continue his investigations into the [*deleted* – little hindrances] lesser misunderstandings that arrive when one nationality tries to unite with another. Not only did he leap the channel in this manner, but on other occasions he took imaginative flights into the upper reaches of society. He would buy himself a white peaked cap & a white suit and walk briskly up and down the promenade until he believed that he was the millionaire owner of a yacht, and the glances of the passers by in which he read envy and admiration enabled him to sense the joys of power and affluence and the [*deleted* – difficulty of] temptation of never relinquishing them . . . Most daring of all, he bought a pair of white spats, an article of wear regarded with much loathing on I.L.P. platforms of that date, & he wore them during a whole summer watching anxiously, I feel sure, to see if his revolutionary [*deleted* – sentiments] ideals were becoming [*deleted* – tainted] damaged thereby . . . Moreover when he was a foreigner it was not always a Frenchman. Sometimes he was a Russian, & sometimes a Welshman from the country, with a little English & a great fund of astonishment at the absurdities of the English temperament. But it is as a Frenchman I remember him best, for once in Penzance where he had made the acquaintance of an English admiral who fortunately knew no French, I came upon this admiral striding down the esplanade in a terrible rage, while my father following, all volubility and gesticulation, tried to convince him that the French had won the battle of Trafalgar.[90]

Intrigued by the complexities of class and ethnic difference, Edward Edwards tested the extent to which he could adopt and discard not only a different class identity, but a different national identity, judging the varying ways in which people reacted to him depending on the characteristics that he presented to them. His choice of historical event to reinterpret on the occasion described above is also indicative of a subversive intent: to question Admiral Lord Nelson's status as a patriotic hero and the significance of his success in defending Britain from French invasion by Napoleon's navy indicates an awareness of national pride in military conflicts and an understanding of the role of imperialism in nationalist discourse. The English admiral's reaction to this affront against his national cultural consciousness is unsurprising.

Edward Edwards's mimicry of the English upper classes is clearly subversive in intent. In his seminal volume *The Location of Culture*, postcolonial critic Homi K. Bhabha analyses the effect that such mimicry, conscious or unconscious, can have:

[M]imicry . . . is at once resemblance and menace . . . It problematizes the signs of racial and cultural priority, so the 'national' is no longer naturalizable. What emerges between mimesis and mimicry is a *writing*, a mode of representation, that marginalizes the monumentality of history, quite simply mocks its power to be a model, that power which supposedly makes it imitable . . . [the] observer becomes the observed and 'partial' representation rearticulates the whole notion of *identity* and alienates it from essence.[91]

Here, Bhabha is commenting on the writings of India under the Raj, but such theories have significance for any colonized nation. In the 1970s, the historian R. R. Davies argued influentially that Wales exhibited features of a colonial society as far back as the thirteenth century.[92] More recently, postcolonial theory has gained increasing credibility as a viable tool with which to analyse the writings of Wales in both its languages, and the number of publications on the topic reflect the increasing adoption by critics and theorists in Wales of a postcolonial stance. Stephen Knight's *A Hundred Years of Fiction* (2004) and Kirsti Bohata's *Postcolonialism Revisited* (2004), for example, analyse explicitly Welsh writing in English in the light of postcolonial theory, while *Postcolonial Wales* (2005), edited by Jane Aaron and Chris Williams, considers the implications of postcolonial theory for Welsh history, politics, education, language and culture, along with such (historically) marginalized groups as women and ethnic minorities in Wales.[93]

For Edward Edwards, issues of class and national identity were clearly inextricably linked, and his practice of mimicking another class or nationality in order to question the perceived superiority of the dominant group was a technique appropriated by his daughter in her writing. Just as Edward Edwards adopted and discarded class and national identities during family holidays to test the mettle of his beliefs and the attitudes of his audience, Edwards too takes on the tones and perspectives of social groups other than her own in her fiction in order to deconstruct them.

Edwards had begun to explore issues of cultural mimicry early on in her authorial career. 'The Conquered', collected in *Rhapsody*, is the first story of hers to feature any explicit reference to Wales. Paradoxically, the only Welsh character in the story, Gwyneth, is explicitly associated with conquering forces, suggesting that Edwards's concern is not solely with national difference, but also with class and gender inequalities, and the inextricable relation of these issues to one another.

The tension between subjugated and subjugator, immediately indicated in this story's title, is explicit throughout. The story is narrated from the perspective of a young man, Frederick Trenier, who visits his aunt's home 'on the borders of Wales' (significantly, given that Edwards rarely specifies national locations), where as a child he spent many happy summer holidays with his cousins, Ruth and Jessica (*R*, 45). Frederick makes it clear that there are far more important things that he would like to be doing: 'I must say I went there simply as a duty . . . I took plenty of books down so that it should not be a waste of time', he says (*R*, 45). He considers himself to be an experienced and accomplished young man, culturally superior to his cousins, and expects to find the place dull and restrictive: after doing his 'duty' he intends to move on quickly to his 'proper' holiday (*R*, 45). Frederick indicates his comparative worldliness in a naively arrogant manner, failing to acknowledge the fact that, as a young man, he has far more avenues of opportunity open to him than his female contemporaries:

> [Ruth] remembered far more about what we used to do than I did; but I suppose that is only natural, since she had been there all the time in between, and I do not suppose anything very exciting had happened to her, whereas I have been nearly everywhere. (*R*, 46)

Much to his surprise, Frederick begins to enjoy his stay after meeting Gwyneth, his cousins' Welsh neighbour. Her 'beautiful voice' captures his attention, and he is taken aback to find that she lives up to Ruth and Jessica's warm descriptions. Gwyneth lives in a large house nearby that was built by her grandfather, and its French doors and Japanese prints are suggestive of a complex hybrid of international influences. '[T]hey do not meet many people down there, and I thought they would be impressed with the sort of person I would be quite used to', he says, demonstrating the social snobbery typical of Edwards's male narrators (*R*, 47).

Gwyneth is the sole Welsh character in all of Edwards's published work. Frederick and his family, it is implied, are all of English ethnicity, and Gwyneth's nationality is indicated by virtue of her difference (Frederick describes her as a 'Welsh lady' (*R*, 46)). Yet her profound empathy with imperialists and colonizers is stressed throughout the tale. Her home is surrounded by Roman roads and scenes of old imperialist battles and, during a walk near her home, she says to Fredrick, 'Just think of all the charming Romans who must have walked here! . . . Does it shock you to know that I like the Romans better than the Greeks?', aligning herself with the dominant power (*R*, 52). In physical appearance, too, Gwyneth has more in common with the stereotypical image of the Romans than the Celts or Ancient Britons: she is 'very tall' with 'very fair hair', and has a regal appearance with a 'really perfect nose' and 'finely carved features, which gave to her face the coolness of stone and a certain appearance of immobility' (*R*, 48, 47). Frederick is rather pleased to discover that the prince consort, a particular friend of Gwyneth's grandfather, had spent a night in the house (*R*, 46).

Attracted perhaps by his sense of her as a social and cultural equal (if not superior), Frederick is initially drawn to Gwyneth, but his infatuation fades as she is increasingly associated in his mind with conquering forces. His disillusionment with her, connected with his preconceived ideas about the Welsh and about women, begins when Gwyneth sings a Welsh song for the family one evening:

> When we got there, right at the beginning of the evening Gwyneth sang a little Welsh song. And I felt suddenly disappointed. I always thought that the Welsh were melancholy in their music, but if she sang it sadly at all it was with the gossipy sadness of the tea after a funeral. (*R*, 54)

We are not told which 'little Welsh song' Gwyneth chose to sing (presumably as the narrator is unfamiliar with Welsh culture he is unable to identify it); he sees the Welsh as mysterious others, with a particular mode of music, and when Gwyneth does not meet these ideas he is disappointed. Her refusal to perform Chopin's anti-conqueror's lament, 'Polens Grabgesang', at his request further frustrates him.[94] This song has great significance for Frederick as it had in the past initiated an evening of political discussion amongst him and his friends. He says:

> I was so much excited about the song, because I shall never forget the occasion on which I first heard it. I have a great friend, a very wonderful man, a perfect genius, in fact, and a very strong personality, and we have evenings at his house, and we talk about nearly everything, and have music too, sometimes. Often, when I used to go, there was a woman there, who never spoke much but always sat near my friend. She was not particularly beautiful and had a rather unhappy face, but one evening my friend turned to her suddenly and put his hand on her shoulder and said, 'Sing for us.'
>
> She obeyed without a word. Everybody obeys him at once. And she sang this song. I shall never forget all the sorrow and pity for the sorrows of Poland that she put into it. And the song, too, is wonderful. I do not think I have heard in my life anything so terribly moving as the part, 'O Polen, Mein Polen,' which is repeated several times. Everyone in the room was stirred, and, after she had sung it, we talked about nothing but politics and the Revolution for the whole evening. I do not think she was Polish either. (*R*, 55–6)

Gwyneth's refusal to sing Chopin's song on the grounds that she cannot sympathize with its patriotic sorrow forces Frederick to realize her imperial associations, and this has the effect of making her appear less attractive to him: 'when I looked at Gwyneth again it seemed to me that some of her beauty had gone, and I thought to myself quite angrily, "No, of course she could not sing that song. She would have been on the side of the conquerors!"' (*R*, 56).

At the same time, Frederick's own position with regards to the conquered is indicative of the superior status that he endows upon himself throughout the story. He claims, as a civilized man, to be aware of the subjugated status of nineteenth-century Poland, but he insists that the attendant lament and sorrow for such a condition be expressed on his behalf by women. He wishes to experience vicariously the deep thrill of profound patriotic sorrow and expects Gwyneth, as a Welsh female, to evoke a quaint, mysterious (but non-threatening) otherland during her performance of her 'little

Welsh song'. Instead, it becomes clear that Gwyneth prefers the spirit and values of his own imperial culture, and has sought to embody them.

The expectation that women in particular will remain true to their ethnic group and its values, even when they are subordinated, is widespread in national discourses. Charlotte Aull Davies has argued that in nationalist movements women have been historically seen as 'nurturers of the nation':

> [Women] have . . . been seen as crucial for the reproduction of the nation, both materially, by giving birth to the next generation of nationalists, and ideologically, by transmitting to them those cultural understandings central to the maintenance of their national identity.[95]

Frederick's expectation of Gwyneth to 'perform' otherness for him, much in the way that other male characters in *Rhapsody* demand that women interpret male creativity through their musical performance, has its roots in power politics. One evening during his stay, Frederick waits in the nearby wood to listen for a nightingale's call:

> I felt that there was nothing I wanted so much as to hear her sad notes. I remember thinking how Nietzsche said that Brahms' melancholy was the melancholy of impotence, not of power, and I remember feeling that there was much truth in it when I thought of his *Nachtigall* and then of Keats. (*R*, 57)

Frederick wants Gwyneth, like the nightingale, to perform for him the 'melancholy of impotence' for both her gender and her ethnic position. Frederick relates to Welsh culture as a 'foreigner': curious, even sympathetic, but unwilling to own or act upon his involvement in its marginalization. In this light, then, Gwyneth's refusal to be melancholy in her performance of her 'little Welsh song' or to sing Chopin's 'Polens Grabgesang', could be read as an act of colonial resistance on both an ethnic and a gendered level. And yet, by identifying herself with the ruling nation, Edwards highlights precisely how Gwyneth has become the conquered.

In the light of Edwards's portrayal of Frederick's response to Gwyneth, Edwards's own refusal to play the role of Garnett's Welsh Cinderella accrues significance, particularly as 'The Conquered' was written before Edwards's London experience. By 1933, while living in the attic room of Garnett's London flat, Edwards was writing explicitly about a people whose colonial status, unlike that of Wales, is uncontested. In an untitled story found in her 1933 diary in the Dorothy Edwards Archive, she describes a young Indian man's awareness of his colonial burden.[96]

The role of the colonized in their own subjugation is central to this story, in which an Indian student, Sukhashean Mitter, visits the home of an English woman, Mrs Fornwood, in order to investigate the possibility of purchasing, on behalf of his uncle, an extensive art collection compiled by her late husband. Mitter explains to Mrs Fornwood:

> My uncle has become rich . . . He wished [sic] to live now in the English style. He was asked to visit an Englishman who had many splendid pictures, so he decided 'Now I too will have many splendid English pictures.' He has entrusted me with the labour of buying them for him, though I do not believe in imitating English manners too much.[97]

Mrs Fornwood, then, is literally the owner of cultural artefacts which Mitter's Indian uncle wishes to acquire in order to aid him in his pursuit of attaining the colonizer's lifestyle, thus becoming 'English' in manners and taste. Mitter's uncle, as a member of a colonized nation, considers the literal ownership of art to be an essential element of the ruling-class lifestyle and wishes to make use of his newly found economic power (he is a successful tea exporter) in emulating his colonizer. In her study of the 1847 report on education in Wales, *The Language of the Blue Books*, Gwyneth Tyson Roberts points out that, like the deliberate attempt to annihilate the Welsh language in Wales in order to reinforce official English rule, the English government also exercised a particular form of linguistic colonization in India with the precise aim of creating 'a class of persons, Indian in blood and colour but English in taste, in opinion, in morals and in intellect'.[98] These people would 'absorb

English values and attitudes along with the language', allowing the colonizers to reach, and manipulate, peoples they may not otherwise have been able to influence.[99] This class of people, made up by those like Mitter's uncle, would become an important operating part of the colonizing machine. Roberts argues: '[t]he successful implementation of this policy would mean that an Indian "class [of] interpreters" would conscientiously devote their working lives to serving the purposes of the power which had colonized them'.[100]

In Edwards's story, Mitter is more politically conscious of his country's conquered status and has reached a point of opposition to it: he is willing to carry out this act for his uncle, who is ready to reject his ethnic background in his pursuit of a perceived cultural superiority, but Mitter himself does 'not believe in imitating English manners too much'.[101] During his time in England, Mitter has become aware of the strategies of power relations used by the colonizer in India, where one culture is given a superior civilized status and the other is dismissed as savage or mysterious, and appreciates the value of his own culture when faced with a dominant alternative. He indicates this via his preference regarding the ethnic origin of the type of women that he considers attractive: 'when he [first] came to England he never admired any but fair women who seemed to him like so many primroses and yellow daffodils. But now he liked dark women better again.'[102]

But Mitter is not straightforwardly a victim of the dominant sociocultural power. In the above passage, Mitter shows at once an awareness of his own oppression whilst simultaneously contributing to the subjugation of others: his ethnically based selection of women to find attractive is a constructed and informed choice, and not a natural and impulsive response. Floya Anthias and Nira Yuval-Davis argue that in national discourse women have historically been constructed as signifiers of ethnic or national difference, suggesting that women 'not only teach and transfer the cultural and ideological traditions of ethnic and national groups [but] [v]ery often . . . constitute their actual symbolic figuration'.[103] Mitter, in his deliberate redirecting of his sexual attention from the 'fair' woman to his own 'dark' woman, is participating in such nationalist articulation of women as literal guardians and reproducers of the nation, bearing his young and raising them in the national tradition, while ensuring the 'purity' of the ethnic line. As Anthias and Yuval-Davis emphasize, '[women] may be required to transmit the rich heritage of ethnic symbols and ways of life to the other members of the ethnic group'.[104] Like Frederick's disappointment at Gwyneth's failure to sing the Welsh song in the manner he expected, or even Garnett's disappointment at Edwards's inability to speak Welsh, Mitter locates his reclamation of his ethnic identity in his relations with women, suggesting that, like his uncle's paintings, women are also key possessions in cultural identity.

In 'Mitter', Mrs Fornwood in effect is acting as one such 'cultural guardian', passing art from one man to another in a move that, despite the new owner's ethnic difference, will perpetuate the perceived superiority of the former owner's culture and values, as well as reinforcing her own marginalized status. In effect, Mrs Fornwood performs a similar role to that of Antonia Trenier in 'Rhapsody' or Leonora Morn in 'Days' as a mere bearer or carrier and not creator or owner of art. But, unlike the women in *Rhapsody*, Mrs Fornwood is offered an opportunity for revenge on her controlling husband and considers taking it. Mitter's suggestion that the pictures are of substantial value brings out 'almost a trace of vindictiveness' in her voice: by selling the pictures that defined her husband, she can reclaim some ground of her own (she decides that if she does sell the paintings, the money will go into an artists' fund in her husband's name, thus obtaining no financial gain herself).[105] By choosing to be buried in its grounds, her husband has tied her to his house forever: 'I should have liked to sell the whole place & live somewhere else but you see we can't', she says, looking at Fornwood's grave, prominently visible from the drawing room window.[106] The beautiful headland above the pebbled bay, where Fornwood's grave sits, looking 'haughtily down at the sea on either side of it', is surrounded by railings, erected by Fornwood before his death, and a nearby sign warns 'Trespassers will be prosecuted'.[107] Fornwood continues to assert his ownership of his home, his land, his culture and indeed his wife, even after his death.

In one of the last stories she ever wrote, Edwards finally makes an explicit link between colonial ventures and the area from which she came. In 'Mutiny', Edwards reveals an intricate awareness of British imperial presence in South Africa, and indeed of British colonialism as a whole, as well as continuing to criticize those seduced by or longing for power. Published posthumously in *Life and Letters To-day* in 1934, 'Mutiny' concerns the return to England of the Reverend Edward Montgomery, a Nonconformist missionary who has spent most of his life working in South Africa. Accompanied by his teenage granddaughter, Primrose, who is visiting Britain for the first time, Montgomery, on board ship on the passage home, finds himself caught up in a sailors' mutiny over food supplies and sleeping conditions. Rather than side with the governing authorities, Montgomery supports the rebellion, able to see the validity of the sailors' cause – a fight against oppression and tyranny – and as a result has attracted the interest of the British press. James Rankin, a reporter from the weekly *Scales Review*, has been sent to cover the story.

Rankin visits Montgomery at Delcage Abbey where he and Primrose are staying with Anthony Delcage, an Anglo-Catholic and member of the landed gentry, whom Montgomery had met in Africa the previous year. Tired of the social pressures of his upper-class lifestyle, Delcage lives alone in a mock Grecian temple on a large expanse of family-owned land where he is waited on only by the occupants of a nearby farmhouse. Despite claiming to have cut himself off from society to live a more natural existence, Delcage cannot help demonstrating the social snobbery characteristic of his class position, as we see in his reaction to the young reporter, Rankin:

> Delcage began to talk to him [Rankin], asking him various questions about political and social personages that he knew . . . It gave Anthony a strange sensation to have that world that he had seen nothing of for nearly a year delineated so completely and yet with a slightly hostile pencil by this undistinguished young man. He terminated the conversation when he had heard enough by getting up from his seat, while Rankin was still speaking . . . (R, 237)

The friendship between the aristocratic, supercilious Delcage and the good-natured, sympathetic Montgomery appears increasingly unlikely to the reporter. Montgomery is grateful to his host but far from reveres Delcage's social standing and lineage, and values instead a more wholesome and simple lifestyle. When discussing his future plans with Rankin, it emerges that Montgomery sees himself as the voice of the oppressed, and plans to continue his missionary work, which he began in South Africa, in another distressed area which has also arguably been impoverished in consequence of colonial processes. He says,

> 'I have not stopped work. I am on my way to South Wales, and after a short holiday I shall undertake whatever labours await me in the distressed areas there.' The young man respectfully applauded this, and they spoke for a while about the schemes for helping the unemployed throughout the country, when Montgomery displayed an extraordinary ignorance, for he was merely setting out blindly with ready hands and broad and still upright shoulders in the direction of the suffering he had heard most about. (*R*, 221–2)

Primrose does not share her grandfather's passion for helping others but instead, like Gwyneth in 'The Conquered', is seduced by the attractions of ruling power.[108] During her stay with Delcage, Primrose becomes increasingly aware of the advantages of living amongst the English upper classes. She undergoes an internal struggle, torn between the influence of her kindly but misguided grandfather and the appeal of Delcage's wealth and social status. As the story progresses, Primrose is increasingly seduced by the perceived superiority of Delcage's type, and attempts to mimic him: 'Prim walked along beside him [Delcage], copying his dignified processional stroll as well as she could, getting nearer to it each minute' (*R*, 226). Montgomery, although readily accepting of Delcage's hospitality, hopes that Primrose will be able to resist the material attractions of Delcage's ruling-class status, and in prayer he 'begged that those who have allowed their hearts to become set upon high places and the temptations of the world might be brought back to the path of grace' (*R*, 233).

For all its colonial references, 'Mutiny' is essentially about Primrose and her attempts to emulate the upper classes in order to win Delcage's approval and ultimately his title; its concerns are very much shared with 'Summer-time', in that a young woman has left school and needs to find her way in the world, but has very few options open to her. Edwards is critical of the social structures that compel Primrose to behave in such a way, describing her as vulnerable in her oscillations between naivety and attempts at sophistication: 'in the expression on her face and her whole attitude, a desire to be impressive and disdainful struggled for mastery with what must have been a natural simplicity and naive enthusiasm for quite child-like things' (*R*, 220). The eponymous mutiny, then, is not that on board the ship, but Primrose's rejection of her grandfather's values. Her internal struggle is evident when Montgomery asks her to walk with him, in order to avoid leaving her alone with Delcage:

> Montgomery went up to her and put his hand with undue earnestness upon her shoulder. 'I would like you to come. It would do you good,' he said, and this was a request and a command too.
> She was on the point of putting down her book and coming; she looked up at him. But suddenly a cold expression came for a moment into her eyes. 'I would rather stay here and read,' she said with decision, and the effect was just as if she had shaken his hand from her shoulder. (*R*, 237–8)

Although she finally evades her grandfather's influence, she does this only by marrying Delcage, and adopting the social power that he represents. Like Gwyneth, Primrose both resists and internalizes the power politics dominant in patriarchal society. But the very manner in which her resistance manifests itself shows that she is also 'conquered' – by the appeals of the ruling class, as well as by her dependent status as a woman.

Both 'Mitter' and 'Mutiny' represent a return to the critique of gender, class and ethnic power struggles embedded in her society that Edwards first investigated in 'The Conquered' in 1926. Rather than aspiring to an English identity in failing to describe industrial Wales in her fiction, as some critics and contemporaries alike have suggested, Edwards in fact, like her father, takes 'imaginative flights into the upper reaches of society' in order to test the strength of her own ideology.[109] As Diana Wallace has suggested in her analysis of female authors using a male narrative voice,

> [F]or women writers, the chance to use a male protagonist can be both liberating and even dangerously pleasurable . . . Writing, perhaps more than any other art form except drama, can offer the writer the imaginative experience of 'being' the opposite sex – or of 'divining' it.[110]

In the same sense, this can also offer the imaginative experience of 'being' the other class (upper) or nationality (English). Just as Edward Edwards relished the opportunity to masquerade as another class or nationality during family holidays in order to test the mettle of his socialist beliefs and also the perceptions of others, so his daughter similarly journeys into the world of the 'other'. Edwards in her fiction employs and deconstructs gender, class and ethnic hierarchies to devalue the establishment that she has mirrored, proving that claims of birth, upbringing or heritage are void. Far from ignoring Welsh issues, then, Edwards's attention in her writing is, in fact, focused on questions of power imbalance and cultural imperialism which she sees as pervasive in Welsh society, as they have been and are in other previously conquered or colonized nations, long after the passing of any formal manifestation of legislative colonization. These stories signal a significant development in terms of Edwards's understanding of the complexities of the gendered, class-based and ethnic power structures that so influenced her view of herself, and indeed of her home country, but which, ultimately, her material circumstances and state of mind could not sustain.

Notes

I

1 Dorothy Edwards, 'On writing', *Cap and Gown*, 23, 1 (1925), 11.
2 S. Beryl Jones, 'Dorothy Edwards as a writer of short stories, *Welsh Review*, 7 (1948), 187.
3 Glyn Jones, *The Dragon Has Two Tongues: Essays on Anglo-Welsh Writers and Writing* (London: Dent, 1968), p. 56n.
4 Deirdre Beddoe, 'Images of Welsh women', in Tony Curtis (ed.), *Wales: the Imagined Nation* (Bridgend: Poetry Wales Press, 1986), p. 227.
5 Glyn Jones, letter to Luned Meredith, 14 December 1985. Courtesy of Luned Meredith.
6 Jones, *The Dragon Has Two Tongues*, p. 56n.
7 Katie Gramich, 'Gorchfygwyr a chwiorydd: storïau byrion Dorothy Edwards a Kate Roberts yn y dauddegau', in M. Wynn Thomas (ed.), *DiFfinio Dwy Lenyddiaeth Cymru* (Cardiff: University of Wales Press, 1995), pp. 83–4, my translation.
8 Tony Brown, 'The ex-centric voice: the English-language short story in Wales', *North American Journal of Welsh Studies*, 1, 1, (2001), 34.
9 Allen Raine was the pseudonym of Welsh novelist Anne Adaliza Beynon Puddicombe (1836–1908), who published eleven novels and a collection of short stories. See Meic Stephens (ed.), *The New Compan ion to the Literature of Wales* (Cardiff: University of Wales Press, 1998), pp. 611–12.
10 John Harris, 'Queen of the Rushes', *Planet*, 97 (1993), 64, 67.
11 Ibid., 72.
12 Ibid., 64.
13 Dorothy Edwards Archive (MS5085), University of Reading, Special Collections (hereafter DEA); packet 6. Dorothy Edwards, diary entry, n.d. [1933].
14 Huw Daniel (ed.), 'History of the Tynewydd group of schools (1975)', *Ogmore Valley Local History and Heritage Society Journal*, 8, (2007), 16–17. While evidence suggests that both Vida and Edward Edwards knew

at least some Welsh, Dorothy Edwards was raised in an English-speaking household.

[15] DEA; packet 6. Dorothy Edwards, diary entry, n.d. [1933].

[16] Edward Edwards is listed as headmaster of Wyndham Mixed School in 1890; see *Kelly's Directory of Monmouthshire and the principal towns and places of South Wales 1891* (London: Kelly & Co., 1891), p. 381.

[17] Glamorgan Archives (GA), Tynewydd Schools Logbook (E/M/55/6), 8 January 1904, 4.

[18] Ibid., 6 February 1911, 62; ibid., 13 April 1911, 63.

[19] Daniel (ed.), 'History of the Tynewydd group of schools (1975)', 19.

[20] DEA; packet 6. Dorothy Edwards, diary entry, n.d. [1933].

[21] DEA; packet 6. Dorothy Edwards, diary entry, n.d. [1933]. Jackson Stitt Wilson (1868–1942) was a Canadian socialist and Methodist; of Edward Edwards's friends, only Wilson and Edwards himself are missing from historical textbooks.

[22] David Garnett, *The Familiar Faces* (London: Chatto & Windus, 1962), p. 93.

[23] DEA; packet 6. Dorothy Edwards, diary entry, n.d. [1933].

[24] Ibid.

[25] The marriage bar was lifted in 1944. See Deirdre Beddoe, *Out of the Shadows: A History of Women in Twentieth-century Wales* (Cardiff: University of Wales Press, 2000), pp. 119, 143.

[26] GA, Tynewydd Schools Logbook (E/M/55/6), 2 November [1904] and 10–11 January [1905], 14, 16.

[27] '[T]he women's campaign [for pit-head baths] seems to have started when a south Wales delegate conference of the WLL [Women's Labour League] was prompted by Mrs Edward Edwards of Ogmore Vale to promote the issue.' Neil Evans and Dot Jones, '"A blessing for the miner's wife": the campaign for pithead baths in the south Wales coalfield, 1908–1950', *Llafur*, 6, 3 (1994), 14.

[28] DEA; packet 6. Dorothy Edwards, diary entry, n.d. [1933].

[29] Ibid.

[30] Ibid.

[31] Ibid.

[32] Tony Brown, '"A personal isolated odd universe": Dorothy Edwards and her short fiction', in Christopher Meredith (ed.), *Moment of Earth: Poems & Essays in Honour of Jeremy Hooker* (Aberystwyth: Celtic Studies Publications, 2007), p. 141.

[33] Rachel Ann Webb, *From Caerau to the Southern Cross* (Port Talbot: Alun Books, 1987), p. 61. I would like to thank Sally Roberts Jones for drawing my attention to this comment.

34 An entry in Ogmore Grammar School's logbook for January 1916 states, 'Dorothy Edwards secured a Boarders Scholarship at Llandaff (Howell's School)', indicating that Edwards was a pupil at Ogmore Grammar School at that time. Entry in Ogmore Grammar School Log, 1916, 177, quoted in W. A. M. Jones (ed.), 'Extracts from the school logbook: Ogmore Grammar School' (unpublished, 2005).

35 Unsurprisingly, Edwards found Christmas a very difficult period for the rest of her life. In a letter to Beryl Jones she said, 'Oh Lord how I hate Xmas in all but theory'. DEA; packet 1, item 24. Dorothy Edwards, letter to S. Beryl Jones, n.d. [*c*.1925].

36 *Glamorgan Gazette* (Friday 4 January 1918).

37 Ibid.

38 Inscription on Edward Edwards's gravestone, Ogmore Vale cemetery. See plate 2.

39 An entry in the Tynewydd Schools Logbook on 22 January 1918 states: 'Mrs Vida Edwards commenced duties', and on 31 March 1919: 'Mrs Vida Edwards has been transferred to Ely (nr Cardiff) School.' GA, Tynewydd Schools Logbook (E/M/55/6), 22 January 1918, 119, and 31 March 1919, 131.

40 Other Rhiwbina residents included the Welsh- and English-language authors R. T. Jenkins, Kate Roberts, Gwyn Jones, Jack Jones and W. J. Gruffydd, many of whom lived there at the same time as Edwards.

41 Harold M. Watkins, 'Dorothy Edwards', *Wales*, 6 (1946), 43.

42 Ibid.

43 I am grateful to Emrys Evans for this information.

44 David Emrys Evans, 'Introduction' to S. Beryl Jones, *In the Armpit of a Mountain* (Hereford: Lapridge Publications, 1996), p. 5.

45 Luned Meredith, 'Dorothy Edwards', *Planet*, 55 (1986), 55.

46 Watkins, 'Dorothy Edwards', 43.

47 Ibid.

48 DEA; packet 4, item 18. Dorothy Edwards, letter to S. Beryl Jones, n.d. [*c*.1925].

49 DEA; packet 9, item 14 (b). Kathleen Freeman, reference for Dorothy Edwards, 24 July 1925. Freeman was a 'lively and learned translator from the Greek' who wrote 'intelligent detective stories' under the pseudonym Mary Fitt. Gwyn Jones and Michael Quinn (eds), *Fountains of Praise: University College, Cardiff 1883–1983* (Cardiff: University College Cardiff Press, 1983), p. 146.

50 DEA; packet 9, item 2. Gilbert Norwood, reference for Dorothy Edwards, 9 April 1925.

51 David Garnett later speculated that *Rhapsody* had been Thorburn's work, saying: '[A]t Cardiff University College she had fallen under the influence

of a young lecturer who may at one time have been engaged to her. But they had finally broken it off . . . It was when they were together that Dorothy had written the stories in *Rhapsody*. At moments I even wondered if he were responsible for them, for the more I saw of Dorothy the more mysterious they became. But he cannot have been a Svengali with Dorothy as his Trilby, for *Winter Sonata* had been written after he had left the country. It had taken her two years to write.' Garnett, *The Familiar Faces*, pp. 93–4.

[52] DEA; packet 7, item 7. Dorothy Edwards, letter to S. Beryl Jones (with footnote from Winifred Kelly), n.d. [*c*.1925–6].

[53] Ibid.

[54] Watkins, 'Dorothy Edwards', 47.

[55] DEA; packet 3, item 16 (b). Dorothy Edwards, letter to S. Beryl Jones, n.d. [*c*.1920–4].

[56] Watkins, 'Dorothy Edwards', 44.

[57] Ibid.

[58] DEA; packet 3, item 12. Dorothy Edwards, letter to S. Beryl Jones, n.d. [*c*.1925–7].

[59] Watkins, 'Dorothy Edwards', 43–4. But this was by no means the beginning of her authorial aspirations. Edwards, by her own admission, began writing at a very young age; in a letter to Jones, she claimed to have written a novel, 'The Runaways', when she was just five years old; another unpublished story, included in the Dorothy Edwards Archives, seems to have been written when she was a teenager. DEA; packet 4, item 9. Dorothy Edwards, letter to S. Beryl Jones, n.d. [*c*.1925]. See also DEA; packet 12. 'The Spirit of Music', unpublished short story, n.d.

[60] Edward J. O'Brien (ed.), *Best Short Stories of 1926* (London: Jonathan Cape, 1926).

[61] Watkins, 'Dorothy Edwards', 48.

[62] DEA; packet 5, item 15. Dorothy Edwards, letter to S. Beryl Jones, n.d. [*c*.1926]. 'The Conquered' appeared on the first page of *The Calendar of Modern Letters* in April 1926.

[63] Glyn Jones, letter to Gwen Davies, 1985. Courtesy of Gwen Davies.

[64] Gwyn Jones, 'Introduction' in Gwyn Jones and Islwyn Ffowc Elis (eds), *Classic Welsh Short Stories* (1971; Oxford: University Press, 1992), p. ix.

[65] Brown, 'A personal isolated odd universe', p. 143.

[66] DEA; packet 4, item 16. Dorothy Edwards, letter to S. Beryl Jones, n.d. [*c*.1925].

[67] DEA; packet 4, item 33. Dorothy Edwards, letter to S. Beryl Jones, n.d. [*c*.1926]. Many of Edwards's letters to Beryl Jones and Winifred Kelly, written during this trip, indicate that Edwards was accompanied by her

mother. On the travelling, for example, Edwards wrote to Jones: 'We had a comparatively good journey. Mother did not turn a hair.' DEA; packet 5, item 3. Dorothy Edwards, letter to S. Beryl Jones, 23 May [c.1926]. Several letters close with the phrase 'Mother sends her love'; see, for example, DEA; packet 5, item 26. Dorothy Edwards, letter to S. Beryl Jones and Winifred Kelly, n.d. [c.1926]. At other points Edwards describes her mother's activities in Vienna, for example, 'Mother is very good here. She has every beggar she meets on her conscience in case they were wounded in the war & she gives away most of her income.' DEA; packet 7, item 3. Dorothy Edwards, letter to S. Beryl Jones, n.d. [c.1926]. In a letter from Florence, Edwards says to Jones, after inviting her to stay: 'I am sure that Mother would be as pleased as I to have you.' DEA; packet 3, item 12. Dorothy Edwards, letter to S. Beryl Jones, n.d. [c.1926–7].

68 DEA; packet 3, item 11. Dorothy Edwards, letter to S. Beryl Jones, 29 June [1926].

69 DEA; packet 5, item 16. Dorothy Edwards, letter to S. Beryl Jones, n.d. [c.1926].

70 DEA; packet 5, item 27. Dorothy Edwards, letter to S. Beryl Jones, n.d. [c.1926].

71 DEA; packet 3, item 16 (a). Dorothy Edwards, letter to S. Beryl Jones, 12 October [1926].

72 DEA; packet 5, item 26. Dorothy Edwards, letter to S. Beryl Jones, n.d. [c.1926].

73 DEA; packet 5, item 5. Dorothy Edwards, letter to S. Beryl Jones, n.d. [c.1926].

74 DEA; packet 3, item 37. Dorothy Edwards, letter to S. Beryl Jones, n.d. [c.1926].

75 In a letter to Jones, Edwards says: 'I intend to finish the volume before I go away', i.e. before departing for her European trip (see DEA; packet 4, item 20. Dorothy Edwards, letter to S. Beryl Jones, n.d. [c.1926]). However, several letters held in the Dorothy Edwards Archive show that Edwards was in fact still working on the volume while in Vienna. In one letter from Vienna, for example, Edwards says: 'There are two stories ready. One is called Sweet Grapes and the other A Garland of Earth. (DEA; packet 5, item 26. Dorothy Edwards, letter to S. Beryl Jones, n.d. [c.1926]). In this, and several other letters from Vienna, Edwards describes writing 'the long short story', which became 'Days'. See, for example, DEA; packet 1, item 25. Dorothy Edwards, letter to S. Beryl Jones, 25 October [c.1926]. It is unclear where 'A Throne in Heaven' was written, although the fact that Edwards intended to write 'two small [stories] about young people' before beginning 'Days' suggests

that this may too have been written in Vienna. DEA; packet 3, item 25. Dorothy Edwards, letter to S. Beryl Jones, 11 January [c.1926].

76 DEA; packet 12. Contract between Dorothy Edwards and the Calendar Press for a collection of ten stories, dated 20 December 1926. The contract is signed by E. E. Wishart, director of the Calendar Press. The collection, however, was eventually published by Wishart & Co., London. Letters of the time suggest that the editor of *The Calendar of Modern Letters*, Edgell Rickword, was integral in securing Edwards's contract. DEA; packet 5, item 5. Dorothy Edwards, letter to S. Beryl Jones, n.d. [c.1926].

77 Jones eventually left Oxford without finishing her doctorate. I am grateful to Emrys Evans for providing this information. Emrys Evans, letter to Claire Flay, 29 April 2008.

78 DEA; packet 5, item 5. Dorothy Edwards, letter to S. Beryl Jones, n.d. [c.1926]. Edwards's 1928 novel *Winter Sonata* is dedicated to S. Beryl Jones and Winifred Kelly.

79 Ibid. The novel Edwards is referring to here is *Winter Sonata*. In the same letter she also discusses plans for a Cardiff-based novel.

80 DEA; packet 5, item 26. Dorothy Edwards, letter to S. Beryl Jones, n.d. [c.1926].

81 DEA; packet 3, item 11. Dorothy Edwards, letter to S. Beryl Jones, n.d. [c.1926].

82 DEA; packet 3, item 37. Dorothy Edwards, letter to S. Beryl Jones, n.d. [c.1926].

83 DEA; packet 5, item 25. Dorothy Edwards, letter to S. Beryl Jones, n.d. [c.1926–7].

84 DEA; packet 5, item 4. Dorothy Edwards, letter to S. Beryl Jones, n.d. [c.1926–7].

85 DEA; packet 3, item 38. Dorothy Edwards, letter to S. Beryl Jones, n.d. [c.1927–8].

86 DEA; packet 5, item 25. Dorothy Edwards, letter to S. Beryl Jones, n.d. [c.1926–7].

87 DEA; packet 2, item 13.Dorothy Edwards, letter to Winifred Kelly, n.d. [c.1927].

88 DEA; packet 5, item 24. Dorothy Edwards, letter to S. Beryl Jones, n.d. [c.1927–8].

2

1 After its initial publication in the periodical *The Calendar of Modern Letters*, 'A Country House' was included in Edward O'Brien (ed.), *Best Short Stories of 1926* (London: Jonathan Cape, 1926).

2 Clare Hanson, 'Introduction' to *Re-reading the Short Story* (London: Macmillan, 1989), pp. 2–3.

3 Diana Wallace, '"A Sort of Genius": love, art, and classicism in May Sinclair's *The Divine Fire*', in Andrew J. Kunka and Michele K. Troy (eds), *May Sinclair: Moving Towards the Modern* (Hampshire: Ashgate, 2006), pp. 50, 52.

4 Katie Gramich, 'Introduction' in Amy Dillwyn, *The Rebecca Rioter* (1880; Dinas Powys: Honno, 2001), pp. x–xi. The remaining five novels in Dillwyn's *oeuvre* employ a female narrative voice, as Gramich points out, to 'satirise the London life of the rich and leisured which she herself knew very well'. Dillwyn was, again like Edwards, particularly critical of 'the social conventions restricting the possibilities of fulfilment for women': ibid., p. viii.

5 Judith Butler, *Gender Trouble: Feminism and the Subversion of Identity* (London: Routledge, 1990), p. viii.

6 Diana Wallace, 'Ventriloquising the Male: two portraits of the artist as a young man by May Sinclair and Edith Wharton', *Men and Masculinities*, 4, 4 (2002), 327. Emphasis in the original.

7 Margaret Whitford, ed., *Luce Irigaray: Philosophy in the Feminine* (London: Routledge, 1991), 71.

8 In Greek myth a thyrsus is a symbol of phallic fertility carried by the worshippers of Bacchus, the bacchantes. Reference to the figure of the bacchante is also made in 'A Country House' (*R* 35) and *Winter Sonata* (*WS* 121).

9 Beryl Jones had apparently found 'La Penseuse' dull; other letters suggest that Edwards's editor, Edgell Rickword, was equally unimpressed with the story. See DEA; packet 3, item 25. Dorothy Edwards, letter to S. Beryl Jones, 11 January n.d. [*c*.1925–6]. Edwards instructed Beryl Jones, 'Both copies are to be burnt'. DEA; packet 5, item 5. Dorothy Edwards, letter to S. Beryl Jones, n.d. [*c*.1925–6]. However, Jones preserved a copy, which was later deposited in the Dorothy Edwards Archive at the University of Reading, Special Collections. I discovered 'La Penseuse' during my research on the Dorothy Edwards Archive, and it remained unpublished until 2007 when it was included by Christopher Meredith in the 'Library of Wales' edition of *Rhapsody* (Cardigan: Parthian, 2007).

10 DEA; packet 3, item 25. Dorothy Edwards, letter to S. Beryl Jones, 11 January n.d. [*c*.1925–6].

11 'I regret the title a little', Edwards wrote to Jones of 'La Penseuse'. DEA; packet 5, item 5. Dorothy Edwards, letter to S. Beryl Jones, n.d. [*c*.1926].

12 DEA; packet 3, item 37. Dorothy Edwards, letter to S. Beryl Jones, n.d. [*c*.1926].

13 Susan McClary, *Feminine Endings: Music, Gender and Sexuality* (Minneapolis and London: University of Minnesota Press, 1991), p. 151.

14 Ibid., p. 138.

15 Christopher Meredith, '*Rhapsody*'s lost story', in Meredith (ed.), *Moment of Earth: Poems & Essays in Honour of Jeremy Hooker* (Aberystwyth: Celtic Studies Publications, 2007), p. 166.

3

1 DEA; packet 3, item 37. Dorothy Edwards, letter to S. Beryl Jones, n.d. [*c*.1926].

2 DEA; packet 2, item 1. Dorothy Edwards, letter to S. Beryl Jones, 18 January [*c*.1926].

3 DEA; packet 5, item 25. Dorothy Edwards, letter to S. Beryl Jones, n.d. [*c*.1927].

4 DEA; packet 3, item 37. Dorothy Edwards, letter to S. Beryl Jones, n.d. [*c*.1926].

5 Susan McClary, *Feminine Endings: Music, Gender and Sexuality* (Minneapolis and London: University of Minnesota Press, 1991), p. 28.

6 Pauline Clark has a forerunner in 'Days', the nearest story in Edwards's *oeuvre* to *Winter Sonata* not only in terms of style, tone and length, but also chronology. 'Days' features a young working-class girl, Bessie; like Pauline, she is depicted as rather uncouth and unaware of social proprieties. Described as a 'big girl, rather pretty, but a little stupid-looking', she takes a liking to composer Alexander Sorel and proceeds to contrive meetings with him (*R*, 166). Edwards uses a similar character in a later short story, 'The Problem of Life', published posthumously in 1934. Mr Rose is visiting his friend Mr Barron in the country; when hurrying to a dinner engagement, he notices a maid, Rhoda, waiting outside a glasshouse in the garden of the home which he is visiting. The maid is described in similar terms to Pauline and Bessie: she is 'a dark thick-set girl' with 'rather coarse black hair' (*R*, 257). Rose, as he is passing, 'let his hand pass lightly and with a casual air over the front of her dress. She blushed and began to giggle, but he had already walked away.' (*R*, 257)

7 DEA; packet 3, item 30. Dorothy Edwards, letter to Sona Rosa Burstein, 30 August n.d.

8 Diana Wallace, *Sisters and Rivals in British Women's Fiction 1914–1939* (London: Macmillan, 2000), p. 106.

9 I am indebted to Dr Marion Löffler at the Centre for Advanced Welsh and Celtic Studies, National Library of Wales, for this information and

the direct translation of 'Lob des Winters', and to John Koch for facilitating the translation.

10   Dorothy Edwards, *Winter Sonata*, p. vii. According to Löffler it is unclear whether the Middle High German word 'geligen' in the final line means 'to lie' as in to lie down, or 'to lie' as in to tell an untruth. Given the context of the poem, the former seems the most likely meaning. Marion Löffler, e-mail correspondence with Claire Flay, 17 October 2008.

11   Dante Gabriel Rossetti, 'Sonnet LXV. Known in Vain' (1881), reprinted in Dante Gabriel Rossetti, *Collected Poetry and Prose*, ed. Jerome McGann, (New Haven and London: Yale University Press, 2003), p. 156.

12   Ibid., ll. 10–11.

13   DEA; packet 3, item 25. Dorothy Edwards, letter to S. Beryl Jones, 11 January [*c*.1926–7].

14   Dorothy Edwards, 'Hardy's Wessex: the spirit of the landscape' (review of Donald Maxwell, *The Landscape of Thomas Hardy*), *Western Mail and South Wales News* (28 March 1929).

15   Several versions of the myth of Persephone's abduction exist, but little differentiates them other than the duration of the period that Persephone spends underground, and the name of Persephone's abductor: in some sources he is named Hades, whereas others cite Pluton, or Pluto, whose kingdom is called Hades. As Edwards uses the version where Hades is the name of the underworld and not the abductor I too shall refer to this version.

16   See Helene P. Foley (ed.), *The Homeric Hymn to Demeter: Translation, Commentary, and Interpretive Essays* (New Jersey: Princeton University Press, 1994).

17   Mary R. Lefkowitz, *Women in Greek Myth* (London: Duckworth, 2007), p. 101.

18   Gwyn Jones and Thomas Jones, trans., *The Mabinogion* (1949; London: Everyman, 2000), p. 8.

19   Ibid.

20   Ibid, p. 10.

21   Lefkowitz, *Women in Greek Myth*, p. 63.

22   For further discussion on the format of *Winter Sonata*, see S. Beryl Jones, '*Winter Sonata* by Dorothy Edwards – a personal estimate' (unpublished, 1986). DEA, packet 12.

23   W. H. Hadow, *Sonata Form* (London: Novello & Company, n.d. [1896]), p. 2.

24   Ibid.

25   Garnett Family Archive, Charles Deering McCormick Library of Special Collections, Northwestern University Library (hereafter GFA). Dorothy Edwards, letter to David Garnett, 1 June 1931.

4

1   Gerald Gould, quoted in an advertisement for *Rhapsody* and *Winter Sonata, Western Mail and South Wales News* (5 December 1929).

2   Luned Meredith, 'Dorothy Edwards', *Planet*, 55 (1986), 50.

3   David Garnett, *The Familiar Faces* (London: Chatto & Windus, 1962), p. 86.

4   DEA; packet 3, item 6. David Garnett, letter to Dorothy Edwards, 22 November [*c*.1928].

5   DEA; packet 5, item 12. Dorothy Edwards, letter to S. Beryl Jones, n.d. [*c*.1929].

6   Dorothy Edwards, letter to David Garnett, n.d. [*c*.1928]. Quoted in Garnett, *The Familiar Faces*, p. 86.

7   DEA; packet 7, item 11. David Garnett, letter to Dorothy Edwards, 4 January 1929.

8   Garnett, *The Familiar Faces*, p. 87.

9   Ibid., p. 89.

10 Ibid., p. 94.

11 Ibid., p. 88.

12 DEA; packet 3, item 5. David Garnett, letter to Dorothy Edwards, n.d. [*c*.1929].

13 DEA; packet 3, item 10. Dorothy Edwards, letter to S. Beryl Jones, n.d. [*c*.1929].

14 Garnett, *The Familiar Faces*, p. 92.

15 DEA; packet 3, item 17 (b). Dorothy Edwards, letter to Winifred Kelly and S. Beryl Jones, 29 April [*c*.1929].

16 David Garnett (ed.), *Carrington: Letters and Extracts from her Diaries* (London: Jonathan Cape, 1970), p. 390.

17 DEA; packet 7, item 13. Dora Carrington, letter to Dorothy Edwards, n.d. [*c*.1929–32].

18 DEA; packet 3, item 29 (a). Dorothy Edwards, letter to Winifred Kelly and S. Beryl Jones, n.d. [*c*.1929–32].

19 Frances Partridge, *Memories* (London: Gollancz, 1981), pp. 76–7. My emphasis.

20 Garnett, *The Familiar Faces*, p. 88.

21 Ibid., pp. 92–3.

22 DEA; packet 2, item 17 (b). Dorothy Edwards, letter to Winifred Kelly and S. Beryl Jones, n.d. [*c*.1932–3].

23 DEA; packet 3, item 29 (a). Dorothy Edwards, letter to Winifred Kelly and S. Beryl Jones, n.d. [*c*.1929–32]. Herbert Henry Asquith was prime minister from 1908 to 1916.

24   DEA; packet 3, item 17 (b). Dorothy Edwards, letter to Winifred Kelly and S. Beryl Jones, 29 April [c.1929].

25   DEA; packet 2, item 2. Dorothy Edwards, letter to Winifred Kelly and S. Beryl Jones, 4 September [c.1929].

26   Beryl Jones has commented on Garnett's account of Edwards '[t]o an old fellow student this is just laughable'. DEA; packet 11, item 1. S. Beryl Jones, letter to Virago Press, September 1986.

27   Garnett, *The Familiar Faces*, p. 87.

28   Stephen Knight, 'Welsh fiction in English as postcolonial literature', in Jane Aaron and Chris Williams (eds), *Postcolonial Wales* (Cardiff: University of Wales Press, 2005), p. 159.

29   DEA; packet 2, item 2. Dorothy Edwards, letter to Winifred Kelly and S. Beryl Jones, 4 September [c.1929].

30   DEA; packet 3, item 19. Dorothy Edwards, letter to Winifred Kelly, n.d. [c.1930].

31   DEA; packet 3, item 17 (b). Dorothy Edwards, letter to Winifred Kelly and S. Beryl Jones, 29 April [c.1929].

32   DEA; packet 5, item 21. Dorothy Edwards, letter to S. Beryl Jones and Winifred Kelly, 2 December [c.1928–33].

33   Harold M. Watkins, 'Dorothy Edwards', *Wales*, 6 (1946) , 45.

34   Dorothy Edwards, letter to Saunders Lewis, 22 October 1931. Quoted in Katie Gramich, 'Gorchfygwyr a chwiorydd: storïau byrion Dorothy Edwards a Kate Roberts yn y dauddegau', in M. Wynn Thomas (ed.), *DiFfinio Dwy Lenyddiaeth Cymru* (Cardiff: University of Wales Press, 1995), p. 81.

35   DEA; packet 2, item 17 (b). Dorothy Edwards, letter to Winifred Kelly and S. Beryl Jones, n.d. [c.1932–3].

36   GFA. Dorothy Edwards, letter to David Garnett, 27 November 1928.

37   Garnett, *The Familiar Faces*, p. 86.

38   DEA; packet 1, item 1. David Garnett, letter to Dorothy Edwards, 13 November 1932.

39   Garnett, *The Familiar Faces*, p. 86.

40   Dorothy Edwards, letter to David Garnett, n.d. [c.1928–9]. Quoted in Garnett, *The Familiar Faces*, p. 86.

41   Fellow Welsh writer Rhys Davies recalls in his autobiography, *Print of a Hare's Foot*, his experiences as a Welshman in London: 'I found among the English an indulgent dismissal of Wales . . . The native language was a joke . . . the Welsh, like the Scottish and Irish, were expected to be idiosyncratic and, better still, amusing': Rhys Davies, *Print of a Hare's Foot* (1969; Bridgend: Seren, 1998), p. 113.

42   DEA; packet 1, item 7. David Garnett, letter to Dorothy Edwards, 14 January 1931.

43   Ibid.
44   GFA. Dorothy Edwards, letter to David Garnett, 9 October 1932.
45   DEA; packet 5, item 19. Dorothy Edwards, letter to S. Beryl Jones and
      Winifred Kelly, n.d. [c.1928–32].
46   DEA; packet 2, item 17 (a). Dorothy Edwards, letter to S. Beryl Jones
      and Winifred Kelly, 4 April [c.1932–3].
47   DEA; packet 2, item 17 (b). Dorothy Edwards, letter to Winifred Kelly,
      n.d. [c.1932–3].
48   DEA; packet 3, item 21. Dorothy Edwards, letter to S. Beryl Jones and
      Winifred Kelly, n.d. [c.1932]. As Tony Brown has suggested, it was
      perhaps as a result of this refusal and the difficulties that it caused her
      that Edwards made the following comment on Mary Baker Eddy,
      founder of Christian Science: '[her] undoubted religious genius is too
      typically American not to appear irresistibly comic from this side of
      the Atlantic, but who, like all Americans who have attempted any spirit-
      ual achievement, did so in an isolation ghastly and utterly impossible
      for a European to conceive of': Dorothy Edwards, 'Famous women:
      figures in history and romance' (review of H. E. Wortham, *Three Women:
      St. Teresa, Madame de Choiseul, Mrs Eddy*; *Diary of St. Helena. The Journal
      of Lady Malcolm*; Marjorie Bowen, *The Third Mary Stuart*; Flora Annie
      Steel, *The Garden of Fidelity. The Autobiography of Flora Annie Steel*),
      Western Mail and South Wales News (14 November 1929). See also Tony
      Brown, '"A personal isolated odd universe": Dorothy Edwards and her
      short fiction', in Christopher Meredith (ed.), *Moment of Earth: Poems &
      Essays in Honour of Jeremy Hooker* (Aberystwyth: Celtic Studies Publications,
      2007), p. 145.
49   DEA; packet 3, item 30. Dorothy Edwards, letter to Sona Rosa Burstein,
      30 August [c.1930–2].
50   During 1928–32, Edwards regularly undertook review work on behalf
      of the *Western Mail and South Wales News*; according to Tony Brown,
      she published thirty reviews during this period. Brown, 'A personal
      isolated odd universe', p. 145 n.; the Dorothy Edwards Archive contains
      a payslip to Dorothy Edwards from Glamorgan County Council Edu-
      cation Committee in payment for an evening class in Rhiwbina, dated
      25 January 1933. DEA; packet 2, item 9.
51   DEA; packet 2, item 2. Dorothy Edwards, letter to S. Beryl Jones and
      Winifred Kelly, 4 September [c.1929].
52   GFA. Dorothy Edwards, letter to David Garnett, 9 October 1932.
53   Richard Garnett, the elder of Garnett's sons, was in boarding school
      at this time, but William Garnett, the younger boy, was in a local day
      school. Richard Garnett recalls that Edwards and his younger brother
      William spent much time together but Richard himself had only a few

brief meetings with Edwards. I am indebted to Richard Garnett for this information.

54 DEA; packet 3, item 18 (a). Dorothy Edwards, letter to Winifred Kelly and S. Beryl Jones, n.d. [c.1933].

55 DEA; packet 3, item 18 (a). Dorothy Edwards, letter to Winifred Kelly and S. Beryl Jones, n.d. [c.1933].

56 Ibid.

57 An entry in Garnett's pocket diary dated 20 January 1933 reads 'Dorothy arrives'. David Garnett, diary entry, 20 January 1933. Courtesy of Richard Garnett.

58 DEA; packet 3, item 15. Dorothy Edwards, letter to Winifred Kelly and S. Beryl Jones, n.d. [1933].

59 Ibid.

60 Ibid.

61 Watkins, 'Dorothy Edwards', 49.

62 DEA; packet 5, item 23. Dorothy Edwards, letter to S. Beryl Jones, n.d. [c.1933].

63 DEA; packet 2, item 16. Dorothy Edwards, letter to Winifred Kelly and S. Beryl Jones, n.d. [1933].

64 DEA; packet 3, item 18 (b). Dorothy Edwards, letter to Winifred Kelly and S. Beryl Jones, 14 February [1933].

65 DEA; packet 3, item 15. Dorothy Edwards, letter to Winifred Kelly and S. Beryl Jones, n.d. [1933].

66 Garnett, *The Familiar Faces*, p. 88.

67 Ibid., p. 96.

68 Ibid., p. 91.

69 Ibid., p. 96.

70 DEA; packet 3, item 18 (b). Dorothy Edwards, letter to Winifred Kelly and S. Beryl Jones, 14 February [1933].

71 DEA; packet 2, item 16. Dorothy Edwards, letter to Winifred Kelly and S. Beryl Jones, n.d. [1933].

72 The Dorothy Edwards Archive includes a copy of a contract between Dorothy Edwards and Wishart & Co., dated 28 December 1933, for a collection of short stories. DEA; packet 8.

73 Garnett, *The Familiar Faces*, p. 97.

74 While Wilson and Edwards shared a correspondence during the 1930s, there is no evidence to suggest that Wilson felt anything more than a sense of paternal affection for the daughter of his old friend; Edwards, on the other hand, developed a preoccupation with him verging on the obsessive.

75 DEA; packet 6. Dorothy Edwards, diary entry, 10 August [1933].

76 DEA; packet 6. Dorothy Edwards, diary entry, 4 August [1933].

77 DEA; packet 3, item 22. Dorothy Edwards, letter to Winifred Kelly and S. Beryl Jones, 1 September [c.1933].

78 DEA; packet 6. Dorothy Edwards, diary entry, 9 September 1933. The irony of her final sentence in this extract, written not quite four months before she took her own life, is striking.

79 DEA; packet 3, item 27. Dorothy Edwards, letter to Winifred Kelly and S. Beryl Jones, n.d. [c.1933].

80 Glamorgan Gazette, 12 January 1934.

81 DEA; packet 3, item 18 (b). Dorothy Edwards, letter to Winifred Kelly and S. Beryl Jones, 14 February [c.1933].

82 DEA; packet 3, item 14. Dorothy Edwards, letter to Winifred Kelly and S. Beryl Jones, n.d. [c.1933].

83 Cardiff Times, 13 January 1934.

84 Edwards was cremated on the following Tuesday at 2.30 p.m. in Glyntaff, Pontypridd, and her ashes scattered on an unmarked plot. The circumstances surrounding Edwards's death are taken from reports in the Western Mail and South Wales News, 10 January 1934, 8, the Glamorgan Gazette, 12 January 1934, 8, and Watkins, 'Dorothy Edwards', 49–50.

85 This similarity has also been pointed out by Christopher Meredith in 'Rhapsody's lost story', in Meredith (ed.), Moment of Earth: Poems & Essays in Honour of Jeremy Hooker (Aberystwyth: Celtic Studies Publications, 2007), p. 170.

86 GFA. Vida Edwards, letter to David Garnett, 12 January 1934.

87 GFA. Vida Edwards, letter to Ray Garnett, n.d. [1934].

88 Glyntaff Crematorium records.

89 DEA; packet 6. Dorothy Edwards, diary entry, n.d. [1933].

90 Ibid.

91 Homi K. Bhabha, The Location of Culture (1994; London: Routledge, 2003), pp. 86–9.

92 R. R. Davies, 'Colonial Wales', Past and Present, 65 (1974), 3–23.

93 See Jane Aaron and Chris Williams (eds), Postcolonial Wales (Cardiff: University of Wales Press, 2005); Kirsti Bohata, Postcolonialism Revisited (Cardiff: University of Wales Press, 2004); and Stephen Knight, A Hundred Years of Fiction (Cardiff: University of Wales Press, 2004).

94 'Polens Grabgesang' was inspired by the fiercely patriotic Chopin's grief for his country when an uprising in 1830 by Polish nationalists against Russian control failed.

95 Charlotte Aull Davies, 'Women, nationalism and feminism', in Jane Aaron, Teresa Rees, Sandra Betts and Moira Vincentelli (eds), Our Sisters' Land: the Changing Identities of Women in Wales (Cardiff: University of Wales Press, 1994), p. 242.

96 The original manuscript version of this untitled story by Dorothy Edwards

appears in her 1933 diary (see DEA; packet 6). However, I shall refer to the recently published version of this story for clarity. See 'Mitter', repr. in Lucy Stevenson, 'Two drafts of an unpublished story by Dorothy Edwards', *Welsh Writing in English: a Yearbook of Critical Essays*, 10 (2005), 174–83.

97 Edwards, 'Mitter', 177. The original manuscript version reads 'wishes' rather than 'wished'. See DEA; packet 6. Dorothy Edwards, untitled short story ['Mitter'].

98 T. B. Macaulay, quoted in Gwyneth Tyson Roberts, *The Language of the Blue Books: the Perfect Instrument of Empire* (Cardiff: University of Wales Press, 1998), p. 55.

99 Ibid.

100 Ibid.

101 Edwards, 'Mitter', 177.

102 Ibid., 176.

103 Floya Anthias and Nira Yuval-Davies (eds), 'Introduction', in *Woman, Nation, State* (London: Macmillan, 1989), p. 9.

104 Ibid.

105 Edwards, 'Mitter', 177.

106 Ibid., 178.

107 Ibid., 174.

108 Primrose's background is a hybrid mix of colonial influences. Her late mother was South African and her English father is involved in the South African mines, the conflict surrounding which initiated, in 1899, the South African Wars between Afrikaans and the British incomers. Primrose had, until recently, been a pupil at a boarding school in Bloemfontain, a South African city with a complex colonial history. In 1909, Bloemfontain was the location of negotiations between the British and the Boers, following the South African Wars; the city is also home to the National Women's Monument, a memorial erected in 1913 in remembrance of the 45,000 women and children who died in British concentration camps during the conflict.

109 DEA; packet 6. Dorothy Edwards, diary entry, n.d. [1933].

110 Diana Wallace, '"A Sort of Genius": love, art, and classicism in May Sinclair's *The Divine Fire*', in Andrew J. Kunka and Michele K. Troy (eds), *May Sinclair: Moving Towards the Modern* (Hampshire: Ashgate, 2006) , p. 60.

Bibliography

Prose and poetry

'Vers Libre, written in 1922', *Cap and Gown*, 20, 1 (1922), 27–8.

'A Lullaby', *Cap and Gown*, 22, 1 (1924), 36.

'On Temperatures', *Cap and Gown*, 22, 1 (1924), 27–9.

Untitled poem, *Cap and Gown*, 21, 2 (1924), 14.

'A Country House', Edgell Rickword and Douglas Garman (eds), *The Calendar of Modern Letters*, i (1925; London: Frank Cass, 1966), 436–48.

'La Penseuse' (unpublished, n.d., *c*.1925). University of Reading, Special Collections, Dorothy Edwards Archive (MS5085).

'On Writing', *Cap and Gown*, 23, 1 (1925), 11–12.

'Pas De Maria', *Cap and Gown*, 22, 2 (1925), 19–21.

'The Conquered', Edgell Rickword and Douglas Garman (eds), *The Calendar of Modern Letters*, iii (1926; London: Frank Cass, 1966), 1–11.

'A Country House', Edward J. O'Brien (ed.), *Best Short Stories of 1926* (London: Jonathan Cape, 1926).

'Summer-time', Edgell Rickword and Douglas Garman (eds), *The Calendar of Modern Letters*, iv (1927; London: Frank Cass, 1966), 216–25.

Rhapsody (London: Wishart, 1927; London: Virago, 1986; Cardigan: Parthian, 2007). Parthian edition includes 'La Penseuse', 'Mutiny' and 'The Problem of Life'.

'G. K. Chesterton', in Edgell Rickword (ed.), *Scrutinies* (London: Wishart, 1928), pp. 29–40.

Winter Sonata (London: Wishart, 1928; London: Virago, 1986).

'Mutiny', *Life and Letters To-day*, 9 (1934), 325–46.

'The Problem of Life', *Life and Letters To-day*, 10 (1934), 662–76.

'Mitter', repr. in Lucy Stevenson, 'Two drafts of an unpublished story by Dorothy Edwards', *Welsh Writing in English: a Yearbook of Critical Essays*, 10 (2005), 174–83.

Reviews

'The Balkans: primitive ways and motoring days' (review of M. E. Durham, *Some Tribal Origins, Laws, and Customs in the Balkans*; P. T. Etherton and A. Duncombe, *Through Europe and the Balkans*), *Western Mail and South Wales News* (10 January 1929).

'Four novels by women: reaction to modern tendencies' (review of Catherine I. Dodd, *Scarlet Gables*; Marjorie Terry, *The Continental Courier*; Ethel Mannin, *Crescendo*; Phoebe Fenwick Gaye, *Vivandiere*), *Western Mail and South Wales News* (28 February 1929).

'Hardy's Wessex: the spirit of the landscape' (review of Donald Maxwell, *The Landscape of Thomas Hardy*), *Western Mail and South Wales News* (28 March 1929).

'A quartette: Miss James's retort to the censor' (review of G. B. Stern, *Petruchio*; Anne Parish, *All Kneeling*; Phyllis Bentley, *Carr*; Norah James, *Hail, All Hail*), *Western Mail and South Wales News* (24 October 1929).

'Famous women: figures in history and romance' (review of H. E. Wortham, *Three Women: St. Teresa, Madame de Choiseul, Mrs Eddy; Diary of St. Helena. The Journal of Lady Malcolm*; Marjorie Bowen, *The Third Mary Stuart*; Flora Annie Steel, *The Garden of Fidelity. The Autobiography of Flora Annie Steel*), *Western Mail and South Wales News* (14 November 1929).

Criticism and biography

Anon., 'Dorothy Edwards', *Western Mail and South Wales News*, 10 January 1934.

Anon., 'Dorothy Edwards', *Glamorgan Gazette*, 12 January 1934.

Anon., 'Dorothy Edwards', *Cardiff Times*, 13 January 1934.

Brown, Tony, '"A personal isolated odd universe": Dorothy Edwards and her short fiction', in Christopher Meredith (ed.), *Moment of Earth: Poems & Essays in Honour of Jeremy Hooker* (Aberystwyth: Celtic Studies Publications, 2007), pp. 140–58.

Flay, Claire, 'A brief biography of the author Dorothy Edwards (1903–1934)', *Ogmore Valley Local History and Heritage Society Journal 2005*, 6 (2005), 59–60.

——, 'Conquering Convention', *New Welsh Review*, 77 (2007), 60–6.

——, 'The subversive Cinderella: gender, class and colonialism in the work of Dorothy Edwards (1903–1934)' (unpublished Ph.D. thesis, University of Glamorgan, 2008).

——, 'The subversive Cinderella: power dynamics and cultural imperialism in the short stories of Dorothy Edwards', in Ailsa Cox (ed.), *The Short Story* (Newcastle: Cambridge Scholars Press, 2009), pp. 116–29.

Gramich, Katie, 'Gorchfygwyr a chwiorydd: storïau byrion Dorothy Edwards a Kate Roberts yn y dauddegau', in M. Wynn Thomas (ed.), *DiFfinio Dwy Lenyddiaeth Cymru* (Cardiff: University of Wales Press, 1995), pp. 80–95.

Jones, S. Beryl, 'Dorothy Edwards as a writer of short stories', *Welsh Review*, 7 (1948), 184–93.

——, '*Winter Sonata* by Dorothy Edwards – a personal estimate' (unpublished, 1986). University of Reading, Special Collections, Dorothy Edwards Archive (MS5085).

Meredith, Christopher, 'The window facing the sea: the short stories of Dorothy Edwards', *Planet*, 107 (1994), 64–7.

——, 'Foreword', in Dorothy Edwards, *Rhapsody*, Library of Wales Series (Cardigan: Parthian, 2007), pp. ix–xiv.

——, '*Rhapsody*'s lost story', in Christopher Meredith (ed.), *Moment of Earth: Poems & Essays in Honour of Jeremy Hooker* (Aberystwyth: Celtic Studies Publications, 2007), pp. 159–70.

Meredith, Luned, 'Dorothy Edwards', *Planet*, 55 (1986), 50–6.

Morgan, Elaine, 'Introduction', in Dorothy Edwards, *Rhapsody* (London: Virago, 1986), pp. ix–xxii.

——, 'Introduction', in Dorothy Edwards, *Winter Sonata* (London: Virago, 1986), pp. ix–xviii.

Stevenson, Lucy, 'Two drafts of an unpublished story by Dorothy Edwards', *Welsh Writing in English: a Yearbook of Critical Essays*, 10 (2005), 160–89.

Watkins, Harold M., 'Dorothy Edwards', *Wales*, 6 (1946), 43–50.

Williams, Teleri, '"Women like sibyls" and "whisps of things": the feminine stories of Dorothy Edwards', *New Welsh Review*, 43 (1998–9), 63–6.

Other works cited

Aaron, Jane and Chris Williams (eds), *Postcolonial Wales* (Cardiff: University of Wales Press, 2005).

Anon., 'Edward Edwards', *Glamorgan Gazette*, Friday 4 January 1918.

Anthias, Floya and Nira Yuval-Davies (eds), *Woman, Nation, State* (London: Macmillan, 1989).

Beddoe, Deirdre, 'Images of Welsh women', in Tony Curtis (ed.), *Wales: the Imagined Nation* (Bridgend: Poetry Wales Press, 1986), pp. 225–38.

——, *Out of the Shadows: a History of Women in Twentieth-Century Wales* (Cardiff: University of Wales Press, 2000).

Bhabha, Homi K., *The Location of Culture* (1994; London: Routledge, 2003).

Bohata, Kirsti, *Postcolonialism Revisited* (Cardiff: University of Wales Press, 2004).

Brown, Tony, 'The ex-centric voice: the English-language short story in Wales', *North American Journal of Welsh Studies*, 1, 1, (2001), 25–41.

Butler, Judith, *Gender Trouble: Feminism and the Subversion of Identity* (London: Routledge, 1990).

Daniel, Huw (ed.), 'History of the Tynewydd group of schools (1975)', *Ogmore Valley Local History and Heritage Society Journal*, 8, (2007), 11–29.

Davies, Charlotte Aull, 'Women, nationalism and feminism', in Jane Aaron, Teresa Rees, Sandra Betts and Moira Vincentelli (eds), *Our Sisters' Land: The Changing Identities of Women in Wales* (Cardiff: University of Wales Press, 1994), pp. 242–58.

Davies, R. R., 'Colonial Wales', *Past and Present*, 65 (1974), 3–23.

Davies, Rhys, *Print of a Hare's Foot* (1969; Bridgend: Seren, 1998).

Evans, Neil and Dot Jones, '"A blessing for the miner's wife": the campaign for pithead baths in the south Wales coalfield, 1908–1950', *Llafur*, 6, 3 (1994), 5–23.

Foley, Helene P. (ed.), *The Homeric Hymn to Demeter: Translation, Commentary, and Interpretive Essays* (New Jersey: Princeton University Press, 1994).

Garnett, David, *The Familiar Faces* (London: Chatto & Windus, 1962).

—— (ed.), *Carrington: Letters and Extracts from her Diaries* (London: Jonathan Cape, 1970).

Gramich, Katie, 'Introduction', in Amy Dillwyn, *The Rebecca Rioter* (1880; Dinas Powys: Honno, 2001).

Hadow, W. H., *Sonata Form* (London: Novello & Company, n.d. [1896]).

Hanson, Clare (ed.), *Re-reading the Short Story* (London: Macmillan, 1989).

Harris, John, 'Queen of the Rushes', *Planet*, 97 (1993), 64–72.

Jones, Glyn, *The Dragon Has Two Tongues: Essays on Anglo-Welsh Writers and Writing* (London: Dent, 1968).

Jones, Gwyn and Thomas Jones, trans., *The Mabinogion* (1949; London: Everyman, 2000).

—— and Islwyn Ffowc Elis (eds), *Classic Welsh Short Stories* (1971; Oxford: University Press, 1992).

—— and Michael Quinn (eds), *Fountains of Praise: University College, Cardiff 1883–1983* (Cardiff: University College Cardiff Press, 1983).

Jones, S. Beryl, *In the Armpit of a Mountain* (Hereford: Lapridge Publications, 1996).

Jones, W. A. M. (ed.), 'Extracts from the school logbook: Ogmore Grammar School' (unpublished, 2005).

Knight, Stephen, *A Hundred Years of Fiction* (Cardiff: University of Wales Press, 2004).

——, 'Welsh fiction in English as postcolonial literature', in Jane Aaron and Chris Williams (eds), *Postcolonial Wales* (Cardiff: University of Wales Press, 2005), pp. 159–76.

Lefkowitz, Mary R., *Women in Greek Myth* (London: Duckworth, 2007).

McClary, Susan, *Feminine Endings: Music, Gender and Sexuality* (Minneapolis and London: University of Minnesota Press, 1991).

Partridge, Frances, *Memories* (London: Gollancz, 1981).

Roberts, Gwyneth Tyson, *The Language of the Blue Books: the Perfect Instrument of Empire* (Cardiff: University of Wales Press, 1998).

Stephens, Meic (ed.), *The New Companion to the Literature of Wales* (Cardiff: University of Wales Press, 1998).

Wallace, Diana, *Sisters and Rivals in British Women's Fiction 1914–1939* (London: Macmillan, 2000).

——,'Ventriloquising the Male: two portraits of the artist as a young man by May Sinclair and Edith Wharton', *Men and Masculinities*, 4, 4 (2002), 322–33.

——,'"A Sort of Genius": love, art, and classicism in May Sinclair's *The Divine Fire*', in Andrew J. Kunka and Michele K. Troy (eds), *May Sinclair: Moving Towards the Modern* (Hampshire: Ashgate, 2006), pp. 49–64.

Webb, Rachael Ann, *From Caerau to the Southern Cross* (Port Talbot: Alun Books, 1987).

Archival material

Dorothy Edwards Archive (MS5085), University of Reading, Special Collections.

Garnett Family Archive, Charles Deering McCormick Library of Special Collections, Northwestern University Library.

Glyntaff Crematorium Records, Glyntaff Crematorium.

Kelly's Directory of Monmouthshire and the principal towns and places of South Wales 1891 (London: Kelly & Co., 1891).

Tynewydd Schools Logbook (E/M/55/6), Glamorgan Archives.

Index